Piano and Keyboard

Moving From Beginner to Intermediate Player

Comprehensive Piano and Keyboard Guide to reading sheet music, understanding complex piano terms and intermediate music techniques

Michael Williams

Legal Notice:

Copyright 2024 by Michael Williams - All rights reserved.

This document is geared towards providing exact and reliable information regarding the topic and issue covered. The publication is sold on the idea that the publisher is not required to render an accounting, officially permitted, or otherwise, qualified services. If advice is necessary, legal or professional, a practiced individual in the profession should be ordered.

From a Declaration of Principles which was accepted and approved equally by a Committee of the American Bar Association and a Committee of Publishers and Associations.

Legal Notes:

In no way is it legal to reproduce, duplicate, or transmit any part of this document by either electronic means or in printed format. Recording of this publication is strictly prohibited and any storage of this document is not allowed unless with written permission from the publisher. All rights reserved.

The information provided herein is stated to be truthful and consistent, in that any liability, in terms of inattention or otherwise, by any usage or abuse of any policies, processes, or directions contained within is the solitary and utter responsibility of the recipient reader. Under no circumstances will any legal responsibility or blame be held against the publisher for any reparation, damages, or monetary loss due to the information herein, either directly or indirectly. Respective authors own all copyrights not held by the publisher.

Disclaimer Notice:

The information herein is offered for informational purposes solely and is universal as so. The presentation of the information is without a contract or any type of guarantee assurance. Readers acknowledge that the author is not engaging in the rendering of legal, financial, medical or professional advice. Please consult a licensed professional before attempting any techniques outlined in this book.

The trademarks that are used are without any consent, and the publication of the trademark is without permission or backing by the trademark owner. All trademarks and brands within this book are for clarifying purposes only and are the owned by the owners themselves, not affiliated with this document.

CONTENTS

CHAPTER 01

WHO IS AN INTERMEDIATE PIANO PLAYER

Learning to play piano is an interesting journey marked with distinctive levels or stages of proficiencies and skills. The intermediate level signifies a very crucial stage of development; it is marked distinctively with special abilities that transcends the beginner level but still tending towards mastery of other necessary skills to get to the advance level. It is important to understand that each level of piano playing represents basic skills that are expected to have attained or acquired by anyone who acclaimed to be in such level or category. For rhetoric, an intermediate piano player is one who has gone beyond beginner stage but still honing skills important to navigate the complexities of advance piano repertoire.

To define a level of piano playing, and by extension, classifying one into either beginner, intermediate, or advance level is multifaceted in nature. The multifaceted aspect that is peculiar to an intermediate level player include musical knowledge, repertoire, ear-training, self-direction, practice habit, performance skills, technical challenges, sight-reading, etc. Let's explain these multifaceted levels for intermediate level one after the other.

The first mentioned above is "musical knowledge". Before a piano player can be tagged as an intermediate player, it is expected that such one has very deep knowledge of musical theories and concepts. Understanding and use of musical knowledge of concepts like key signature, time signature, cycle of fifth, etc. are used and navigated through by confidence by such person. Since an intermediate player is expected to be able to read musical sheet with confidence and give the expression of what they read on the piano, they are expected to be well accustomed with the musical theories and be able to deploy the knowledge conveniently.

Also, an intermediate player is one who is confident to play diverse genre of music, they proud themselves with the ability to play diverse repertoire that have in them some range of technical difficulties.

Though they may still be working on gaining more accuracy and flexibilities in playing complex pieces that will be easy for the advance level players, they showcase to a very reasonable degree some level of stability in compositions that are tasking in terms of technicality.

Another one is ability to play by simply hearing. To be qualified as an intermediate pianist/ keyboardist, one must have trained their ears to hear distinctive sounds of piano notes and chords. Since an intermediate player would be exposed to diverse genres of music as stated earlier, they are expected to score lots of songs within various genres they are exposed to, and most times they are going to rely on their hearing ability that built from ear training to get what was played in a music. With efficient ear training, they are able to play simple melodies and harmonies just by hearing new piece they want to play.

The ear training also helps them improve their ability to recognize pitch and melodies in music. The mastery of this skill over the years or months (depending on their growth and progress) lays a great foundation for good development in improvisation and musical exploration.

In addition to this, one of the distinctive features of an intermediate piano player is that they are self- directed. They are exposed to different kind of genre, and so they have experience and have built solid confidence in some genre more the other. They can easily choose musical pieces they have interest in based on their confidence, interest, musical preferences, and goals. Being selfdirected makes the journey more interesting to them since can derive personalized and customized fulfilment from it based on the fact that they themselves are the main persons in control of the journey though they can get advice from their teachers, trainers, or colleagues.

Furthermore, they exhibit a very heightened level of discipline to constant practice/rehearsal. The skills they acquire during the intermediate level require constant practice to horn them, so they can't afford to be slack in consistency to their daily routine. For instance, skills like sight-reading and ear training require consistent practice, so they are most dedicated and daily give some time to rehearse for strategic improvement. This obviously leads to the next point of the multifaceted approach which is the "performance skill".

The consistency with practice would in turn help an intermediate player to be able to performance publicly places, though mostly at smaller scale for some time because they might have not built the confidence enough to perform in public at larger scale. In no time, they develop what is known as stage presence, understand audience management and be able to manage stage anxiety. They also are able to carry their audience along by rendering their performance with elegance mainly at the middle of being an intermediate or towards last part of being an intermediate to the beginning of being an advance player.

To add to these, an intermediate player is one who often encounters technical challenges that demand a great deal of focus as they progress in same level. They are often stuck trying to play a piece accurately, trying to play a piece with perfect interpretation and expressions a musical piece deserves. They are always trying to apply effective phrasing, articulation, dynamics, etc. to a piece.

Their playing patterns strive to move beyond the surface level of just playing the notes like the beginners would do to give more of expression and engaging musical experience to their audience.

More also, another feature of an intermediate player is that they are very well accustomed with sight-reading musical sheets. Before a person can be tagged as an intermediate piano/keyboard player, they are able to read musical sheet easily and play whatever they see in the sheet accurately.

Though sight-reading skill is developmentally, they have reached a certain level of confidence for them to be able to read and make meanings of moderately complex pieces and translating the notes on the pages to coherent musical phrases. They also are very likely to grow and wax strong in the knowledge of harmony. They are easily able to identify simple and moderately complex chord progressions, and structures of harmony built in a musical piece.

They are easily able to identify simple and moderately complex chord progressions, and structures of harmony built in a musical piece.

In summary, an intermediate player can be seen as one who is at the "middle of the sea" of piano mastery. They have gone beyond the mere surface and what we can call the "shallow zone" of beginner level, right into the middle of the piano "learning sea" with a lot more of confidence, challenges, and responsibilities.

An intermediate piano player embodies a stage or level of musical development characterized by a perfect blend and mixture of competency in musical knowledge, technical challenges, self-direction, ear training, diverse repertoire, disciplined practice habit, performance skills, etc. They have grown or are growing with the skills aforementioned.

WHAT MAKES A PLAYER A BASIC PLAYER OR AN INTERMEDIATE PLAYER

It is important to know that piano learning and playing journey is highly transformational in scope. Each level is marked distinctively by certain progress, achievement, characteristics, milestone, etc. Each level (beginner, intermediate, and advance) has intricate differences that distinguish each stage from another. In this exploration, we delve into major comparisons between the beginner level and an intermediate level of piano playing. The comparison and contrast between basic player and intermediate player include various aspects such as musical knowledge, repertoire diversity, ear training, technical knowledge, practice habit, etc. Full understanding of the distinctions between these two stages will help the learners to know things that are expected of them at each level. They are better prepared when they know what is ahead of them.

Knowing the nuances also help both the learner and the teacher to plan and tailor effective and efficient teaching curriculum and strategies to facilitate such smooth progression and development through each level of piano proficiency and mastery.

To begin with the comparison between the two levels, let's talk about the technical proficiency pertaining to the two levels. The first of the required technical proficiency in piano playing is "finger technique". For the beginner level, it is characterized by basic developmental and foundational level in building correct fingering pattern, struggling to build fingering stability, strength, agility, and fingering control. A beginner level piano player has significant routine of exercising with basic fingering patterns as a compulsory way/ method to get acquainted with the keyboard. whereas an intermediate piano player is already acquainted with these basic fingering patterns and have no difficulty in playing different fingering patterns pertaining to different notes, scales and progressions.

In addition to the above, a beginner piano player has big challenge with what is known as hand independence. A beginner piano player usually than rarely struggles with hand independence – hand independence is one of the most challenging aspect of piano learning mostly at the early level of piano learning. They are most likely have to put extra focus and attention to get hand coordination right at this stage/level, and most time they struggle to get the hand coordination right.

Some time, they would be required to play different notes with one hand while they play different notes or usually chords on the other hand; and this often get them confuse most times.

The intermediate piano players on the other hand have passed through this level. They are able to play with both hands and can play either same thing or different things simultaneously with both hands. They run scales easily with either one hand or both hands correctly and smoothly. They play same chords or different chords simultaneously with both hands and are able to even create their own music on their own. They are also able to manage different rhythms and articulations in both hands simultaneously resulting in more smooth and correct expression of intending emotions.

Also, it is important to understand that beginner level piano players only do encounter challenges in the basic fundamental exercises and simple pieces because their scope of knowledge only cover such aspect. They are only introduced to basic and fundamental aspect of piano such as fingering patterns, hands techniques, finger numbers (e.g., C, D, E, F, A, B, C - 1,2,3,4,5,6,7,8), basic hand movement, circle of fifth, etc.

Complex concepts like articulation, ornaments, sight-reading, trills, intricate hand movement, etc., are strange to them or are very difficult to them at this stage. It is only the intermediate player or an advance player can apply or play piano with the application of the aforementioned easily or with lesser difficulty as the case may be.

A beginner level piano player is still at the stage of fingering technique development, while an intermediate level has gone beyond developing the fingering pattern and stability to putting up with enhanced fingering patterns, scales, chords progressions, ability to tackle complex technical challenges that can or may be a great frustration to a beginner player, etc.

In addition to the comparison and contrasting of beginning and intermediate playing level, there is a great difference between the two levels in the area of musical knowledge. One of the significant characteristics of beginner level of piano playing is that players of this stage are at the level of trying to understand and get good/perfect grasp of basic or fundamental music theories concepts. They are yet to have full grasp of concepts like time signature, key signature, cycle of fifth, articulation, sight-reading, etc. They are in the process of understanding most concepts of music and at the stage of building basic skills for further improvement.

They are mostly concerned with touching the right notes while they play piano and may make mistake most time playing wrong note or chords while trying to play simple pieces and songs. They cannot, like the intermediate players, play with expression and articulations. They are often limited to what they see on music sheet if at all they are able to read musical sheets correctly – they cannot play the piano like intermediate players that can add expression, articulation, and dynamism into while playing musical sheets.

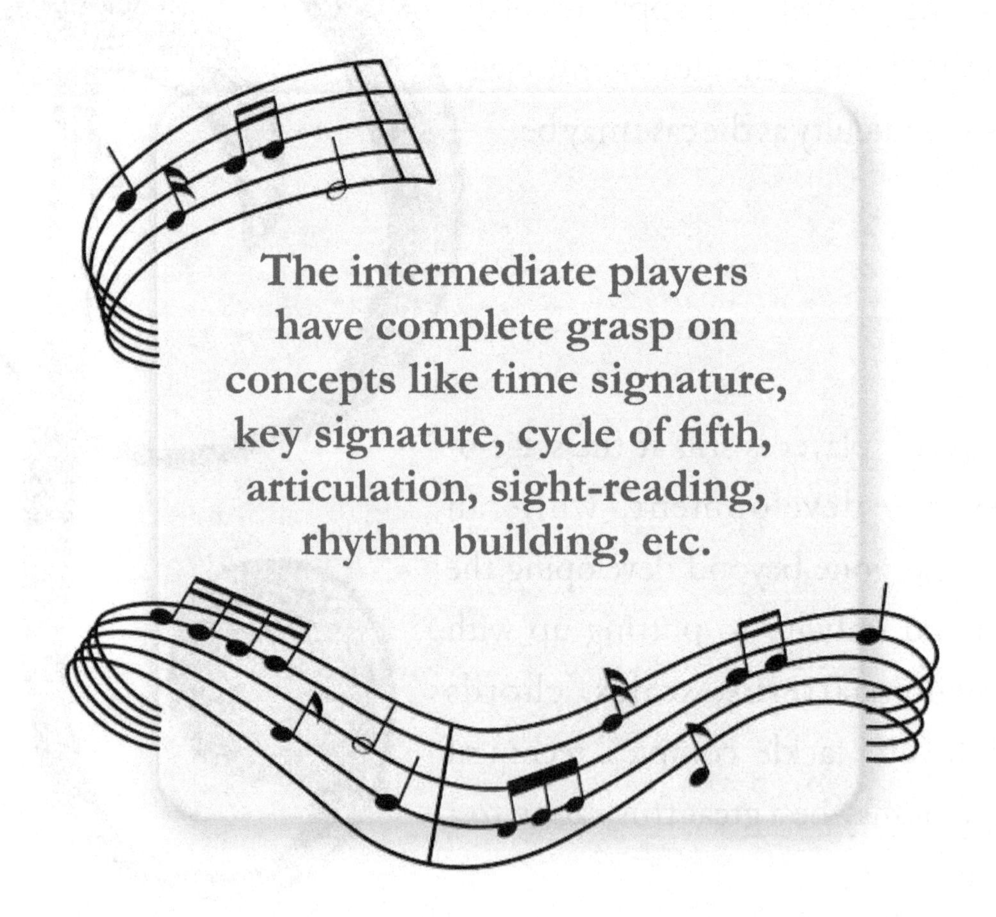

Furthermore, another obvious difference between the beginner piano level and the intermediate level is the level of their repertoire. When we talk of musical repertoire, we mean those diverse genres of music that a player is exposed to and can perform. The beginner level of piano playing is characterized by limited and simple repertoire. They are exposed to simple music and simple pieces rather than complex genres and tasking/complex pieces. The beginner level of piano playing is focused on building simple repertoire that emphasizes basic technical skills alongside fundamental musical concepts rather than complex technical skills and complex musical concepts.

The result of this is that they are kept within the confinement of basic musical styles at the level of their level repertoire. They are in the business of establishing themselves in the foundational understanding of musical theories without interference with complex concepts, theories, and advance/complex genres. The intermediate piano players unlike the beginner piano level players are well exposed to diverse repertoire with range of difficulty levels.

They have broad exploration of diverse and complex repertoire and musical styles. Unlike beginner piano level players, they have holistic and eclectic approach in their choice of music styles such as Jazz, Classical, Pop, etc., and this diversity help them in all-round musical education to bring about musical versatility.

To add to these, there is also significant difference between the beginner level and intermediate level in terms of their practice habits. The beginner level players are on the journey of developing discipline and building permanent habits towards learning the basics and fundamentals of piano.

They are just being introduced to concept of regular routine for practices and rehearsal to get them accustomed with the fundamentals. The beginner level players practices are usually relatively short they are on the journey of building basic techniques and skills that will be the chief cornerstone and solid foundation for their further growth and rapid development. Intermediate players on the other hand exhibit a high level of discipline in terms of their routine practices. They are also accustomed with the fundamentals of piano and they are confident to use these basic knowledges and build on them. Intermediate players are able to move beyond mere practicing to setting of goals on various things like mastery of some technical/complex pieces, development and growth in technical proficiency, they are most engaged in practices that are goal and achievement orientation.

They are able to take initiative of being able to control their speed or pace of rehearsal and are able to relate with and create different rhythms for mastery, they also explore varied genres and music styles that enhance their creativity.

Another disparity between the two levels is area of ear training that is very important to playing by hearing. The beginner level is marked by early stage of developing basic pitch recognition. They are in the stage of developing their hearing ability to recognize basic pitch and melodies in a way to play basic melodies. Because the beginner level is marked with developing habit for pitch recognition, they have limited harmonic awareness and will most likely struggle to have good grasp of chord progression and structures of harmony because their ear is mostly focused on single melodies that are built with single notes. Intermediate players on the other hand have the ability to recognize complex harmony, pitch, and melody. Intermediate players do not struggle to play single melodies. They have strong, heightened, and enhancing capacity to play simple pieces and learn complex ones because of such sensitivity they have in the hearing to sounds of notes, chords, scales. Etc. In other words, intermediate players are equipped to understand harmony and harmonic structures.

Their knowledge cut across identifying basic chord progressions, various harmonic structures, being a contributor in terms of real appreciation of the underlying musical architecture. They are also able to create their own melodies. By this, they are able to explore what is known as improvising method or improvisation – they are being creative with the knowledge they have by creating their own harmony, melodies, progressions, etc.

Another area of difference is the likeliness of variations of performance skills between both levels (beginner and intermediate). Beginner piano players are mostly limited in terms of exposure to performance situation. Public performance by beginner piano players are rare, and even when they occur, they are usually at smaller scale.

Beginner players are still in the process of developing their stage confidence and poise to perform amidst large audience in performance settings.

On the other hand, while it may still be a struggle for intermediate players or simply not being comfortable enough to perform at advance performance settings, they still have the confidence to perform at smaller scale settings, at studio classes, and other informal gatherings serve them as opportunity to showcase their skills and mastery.

Also, intermediate players have overcome stage fright and anxieties in playing amidst smaller scale audience. They have the poise for musical expression and able to carry along their audience by being able to give right expressions to music they play to elicit their desired emptions from their audience

Lastly, it is important to add to the above differences between beginner and intermediate level a more obvious disparity between the two in term of self direction of players in both levels. The level of self direction of both levels differs in the sense that the beginner level players are always depending on their teacher or tutors to give them guides on the genre they are to learn. In fact, the beginner level players mostly often rely on their teachers for choice of the songs they learn and their repertoire in general. Their teachers are saddled with the responsibility of choosing their songs for them based on their level of knowledge and what they are learning at the point in time in a way to match up with their current skills and with the view of helping them develop certain skills.

While the intermediate players have the capacity and ability to choose their repertoire themselves since they are more exposed and well-grounded in diverse genres.

Unlike the beginner level players, intermediate players are able to infuse their personal touch while playing piano. They are able to go creative with piano playing. They are able to give artistic expression to musical sheets they play. Intermediate players are able to take initiative in selection of repertoire and also able to compose music of different genres based on their knowledge of these genres.

WHAT IT TAKES TO BE AN INTERMEDIATE PLAYER

Some of the points here are already being explained under the comparison made in the previous chapter between a beginner level player and an intermediate level player. This is for the sake of emphasis, a way to reiterate, and to give focus to those skills that are necessary for an intermediate player since this book is all about becoming bonafide and confident intermediate piano player – most part may sound like repetition but there is need to understand who you are becoming (intermediate player) after this course, and you should know the level of expertise and skills expected from you to be qualified as an intermediate player.

They have gained so much fingering stability and strength. Intermediate players are those who understand and have mastered different fingering patterns necessary for different scales and have gained both speed and dexterities in their fingering pattern via intense and consistent exercise.

They are already being drilled to the extent that they have gained control over their fingering patterns to gain agility and control over these patterns. In addition to the mastering of the fingering patterns, they have good control over their hands. They are capable to move their hands consciously to wherever they desire on the keyboard. It is important to note that being able to move hands consciously by the intermediate players give them the advantage to be able to play different melodies and harmonies that may be ordinarily be complex for a beginner player. The skill of being able to move hands easily are cultivated through various exercises that are an intermediate player should have passed through.

In addition, it is important that an intermediate piano player has a very deep and solid knowledge of basic music theory concept. It is expected that such a player had mastered reading and playing with concepts like key signature, time signature, and other musical terms (e.g., ornament, scale, articulation, chords, notes, etc.). Understanding these musical theories should transcend beyond knowing them in the theories only, it is expected to influence their playing skills. The knowledge and application of these musical theories should help them in turn to be able to give right interpretations and correct expression to music they play.

An intermediate player is one who has gone beyond only playing correct notes to giving expression and interpretation to music – musical expression becomes their focal point and aim whenever they perform. They are able to interpret music beyond notes to incorporate articulation, dynamics, and expression into music/piece they play to bring out and express desired emotions from and to the audience.

Also, one of the qualities necessary to be called an intermediate player is ability to possess perceptive and fluent sight-read skill. The result of this is confidence to tackle moderately complex pieces. Sight-reading ability enables the intermediate players to be able to develop exponentially in the playing skills since they are/will be able to play pieces from different genres and in turn enlarge their repertoire. One could also notice that intermediate players are more dedicated to practice because the skills they ought to have like this said sight-reading made it a necessity for them. They dedicate so much time to honing the skills expected of their level as intermediate players. Also, an intermediate player is expected to have a definite set goals for their practices.

The intermediate player is dedicated not only to practice but to longer and focused practice in a bit to improve greatly and to be able to master skills needed as an intermediate and to maintain the quality of such skills.

To add to this, it is expected that an intermediate repertoire comprises various range of pieces, diverse styles, and pieces with diverse levels of difficulty. It is expected of an intermediate player to be an explorer of musical compositions from various musical eras and genres. It is expected to have a wide and all-round range of repertoire. The influence of a wide range repertoire is that the player will be solid in musicality and have a comprehensive musical education.

Since the repertoire the intermediate players interact with are mostly challenging, these technical challenges overtime help the development and improvement of their overall skill sets. Overcoming these complexities bit by bit give them confident to explore more styles of music which made them have more eclectic approach to their repertoire selection. This in turn broadens their musical horizon, and made them flexible and adaptable as a piano player.

Furthermore, it is advisable for an intermediate player to demonstrate a great skill of ability to recognize pitch and melodies by ear. Even though the ear-training and the hearing skill is ongoing, an intermediate player should be able to play simple melodies and mild complex melodies by ear. The ear-training they are being subjected to should be enough to help them learn new simple pieces with no or less trouble. It also takes harmonic recognition to be called an intermediate piano player.

With a well-developed ear-training, intermediate players are able to be aware of harmonies, melodies, exploring improvisation, adding embellishment, etc. Their awareness of harmonies is such a great skill that help them being able to tackle complex composition that ordinarily would be difficult for a beginner level player. Also, being able to improvise is a feature of an intermediate player that give them the edge of creativity and musical expression.

To add here, an intermediate player is experienced in more technical aspect of piano playing such as ornamentation, trills, grace notes, accelerandos, ritardandos, and all other tempo variations and dynamism there are.

Lastly, intermediate piano players are set directed individuals that have accrued enough knowledge to a certain level that made them more initiative in selecting wide range of repertoire. While they might be guided by their teachers or tutors at different levels, they are still kind of being autonomous in pieces that align with their goals, musical preferences, learnability, etc. at different stages of their journeys. They practice and learn based on set goals. Their practices have gone beyond learning the fundamentals to learning to achieve a goal or master certain complexities or to overcome certain technical challenges. They are aware of their limitations too, and are able to set goals to overcome them most time via picking musical pieces that have such challenges in a bit to be accustomed to them and eventually learn them and get used to them.

A BRIEF GLIMPSE INTO WHO A PROFESSIONAL PLAYER IS

It is important for you, as a "to be" intermediate player, to know what level is ahead of you. It will (probably) prepare you to be anxious to learn more and pay close attention to this level or stage you are about to study. Note that the successful completion of each level is the key to open door to the next level. Without wasting much of time, who then is a professional player? A professional player is one who can be regarded as a custodian of traditional music in its essence, one who innovates sounds, one who is a custodian of the innovative power that music holds, etc. The journey of a professional piano player is marked distinctively by profound continuous learning lifestyle, musical exploration, and certain unique level of connectivity with the art they bring to life.

There are several characteristics peculiar to them and their musical journey. We are going to consider just few of them. One of these characteristics of these set of people is their mastery of technique. Their mastery of technique firstly as gone beyond mere mechanical execution of notes. They have built fingers strength and agility that aid their hands movement and fingering flexibility on keys. Their fingers are able to dance effortlessly on piano to producing symphony sounds that show that they've gone through years of dedicated practice. Their advanced finger strength and agility makes it easy for them to navigate the landscape of complex musical compositions like Jazz, Pop, Contemporary, and other classical creations with competence. Also, they are custodians of top-notch musical knowledge.

They have deep understanding of theoretical part of music, counterpoints, harmonic chords and progressions, unique composition structures. Their deep knowledge of musical theories enables them having the capacity to go beyond scoring a song to breathing life into a song/piece. Their performance is beyond performance – they tell stories with performances and they are able to evoke their desired emotions from their audience. They create atmospheres and feelings with their performances. They are even able to recreate a song to suit desired situations. They are also able to define performances in their own ways by breathing life to the white and black keys with such a nuance that could be compared with being "divine" or "heavenly".

In addition, a professional piano player can be known by how deep and wide their repertoire is. They are often seen and known to be versatile. They have so much wide range of repertoire that consist complex works from different genres. Their diversity is a testament of their versatility. They are so versatile to the extent that their repertoire showcases as evident how easy it is for them to sail or manipulate through various genres and styles without losing grip of their professionality and artistic probity. It is also important to note that professional players are characterized with rigorous practice routine by giving so much time to horning their skills daily. We can simply say they are well disciplined in terms of practices/rehearsals they subject themselves to achieve certain levels of professionality and playing skills.

Also, we have to talk about the advanced hearing skill and musical sensitivity these people have. They have trained their ears to the extent that they can play virtually every song by ear. They have gone through a very refined ear training to be able to do so.

They are able to recognize by ear melodies, harmonies, progressions, etc. This ability gives them the ability to play beyond technicalities there in a music to connecting with their audience emotions. Their ears become a very dependable guide responding for compassing them through the expressive of nuances of pieces they play.

They have such an artistic identity that is not confined to the works of others. They seek to have identity that are unique instead of being confined to the work of others. They respect the works of others, but they are sure to create or infuse their personal touch always as a means to stand out from the crowd.

Furthermore, a professional piano player is one who has mastered the art of public performance. They are able to performance on larger scale and are able to connect with their audience easily with music they play. On the stage, they are able to command the audience attention and also command the hearts of their audiences. They engage their audiences on stage with music that transcend mere physical playing to evoking of thoughts and emotions in a manner of journey revealing through every note they play. They are able to create expressions with music on stage.

Beyond stage performance, they become major contributors to musical community by adding value to musical community via various means. Some of the professional players work as educators or tutors and help in passing across knowledge to the younger generations. Some also become partners with other musicians to create refining aesthetical landscape of Piano playing. They are able to influence the music world around them by their knowledge and experience.

CHAPTER 02

INTENSIVE DISCOURSE ON CHORDS

In the previous book for the beginner piano players, we have discussed briefly on chords and even gave a few examples on it. You will recur when you studied chord at beginner level that we referred to a chord as a set of 2 or 3 notes played simultaneously or nearly so. We said that to you because you are at the beginner stage and we only dealt with simple chords then: major chords, minor chords, diminished chords, and augmented chords – these are the triads we have in piano chords. Don't forget that the word "triads" is from the word "three". It will interest you that a chord can be more than combinations of the 2 or 3 notes we thought you earlier.

It will interest you that a chord can even consists up to 5 notes. For this level, we will like to modify the definition of what a chord is so that you won't get confuse as we proceed in this chapter. A chord is explained as playing many notes that have harmonic relationship together. Or a chord is harmonic set of pitches of notes that are played together simultaneously or almost so.

It is also important that you know and understand some basic terms that we may usually encounter in this chapter. The first is what is known as "root". When we say root or root note, we refer to the note on which certain chord is built on. For instance, the root of Cmaj7 Chord will be note C. Another one is known as "broken". When we say a chord is broken, we mean they are played separately – they are not played together simultaneously. It means they are played apart.

We also have a term known as "solid". Solid is the actual opposite of broken. It simply means that all the notes that made up the chord are played together at same time. The last of these common terms that are frequently use when talking about chords is called "inversion". Inversion is changing or reordering of notes in a chord stack. Note that when the chord is inverted, the root note cannot longer be at the start or bottom of the stack of the chord anymore. Let's now dive in to explain each chord intensively with copious examples. You are advised to learn these chords and dedicate time to practice them and score recommended songs under each chord explanation.

In the previous book for the beginner piano players, we have discussed briefly on chords and even gave a few examples on it. You will recur when you studied chord at beginner level that we referred to a chord as a set of 2 or 3 notes played simultaneously or nearly so. We said that to you because you are at the beginner stage and we only dealt with simple chords then: major chords, minor chords, diminished chords, and augmented chords – these are the triads we have in piano chords.

Don't forget that the word "triads" is from the word "three". It will interest you that a chord can be more than combinations of the 2 or 3 notes we thought you earlier. It will interest you that a chord can even consists up to 5 notes. For this level, we will like to modify the definition of what a chord is so that you won't get confuse as we proceed in this chapter. A chord is explained as playing many notes that have harmonic relationship together. Or a chord is harmonic set of pitches of notes that are played together simultaneously or almost so.

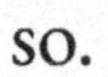

Triads

With the name above, we can easily suggest what number of notes to realize chords under this category. Triads are chords that are made up of 3 notes. However, some players may sometimes play triads with addition of their root notes at the end of the triad to realize 4 notes. Chords realized as such are still regarded as triads.

Example of a triad chord in diagram

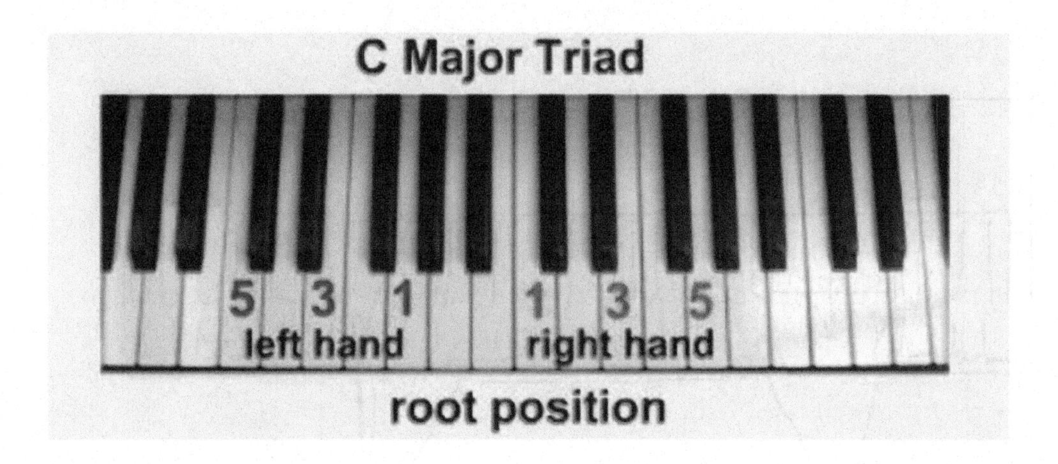

Chords under this category are referred to as basic chords. They are: major chords, minor chords, diminished chords, and augmented chords. Let us discuss these basic chords one after the other with copious examples.

Major Chords

Major chords are known widely as the simplest and most common type of chords. Major chords are also known or popularly called "happy chords" because they sound happy. They are usually built on the first, third, and fifth notes of the major scale. These three notes are professional tagged as the root, major third, and perfect fifth. The structure of these chords follows a specific intervallic structure that we follow to create these chords. The structures are as follow: root to major third (Rm3), major third to perfect fifth (M-P5).

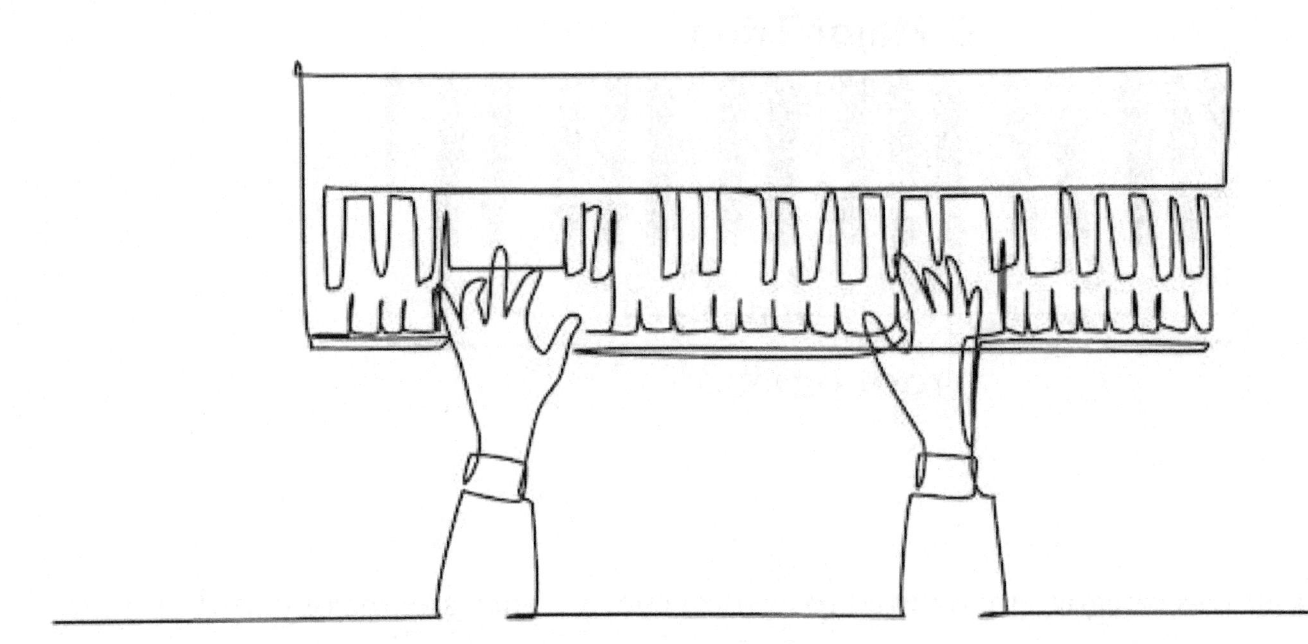

Description, diagram and pictorial representation of major (chords) triads in ascending order from C

C Major Triad

C Major chord is the most popular of the chords on piano. The construction of the C major consists three notations which are C, E, and G. C is the root note, E is the major third, and G is the perfect 5th

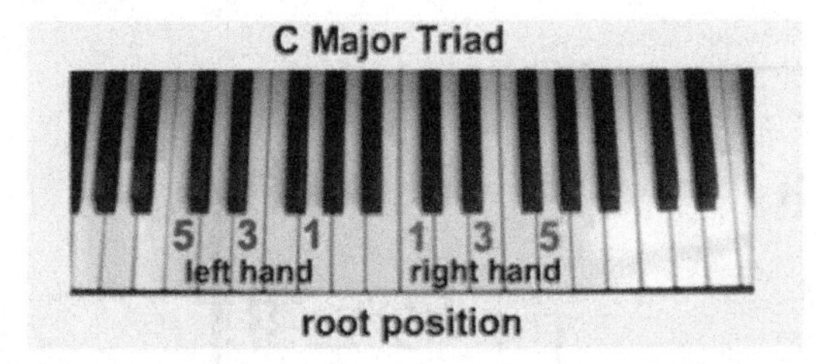

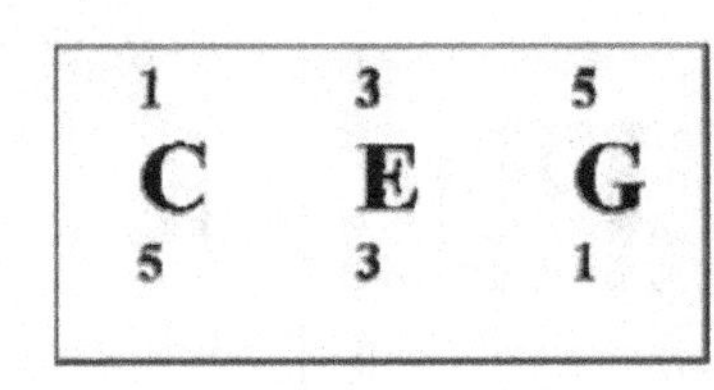

The above images are pictorial representations of C major chord on a piano, musical chat, and music sheet.

Examples of popular songs that were composed on C Major Chord.

1. "No woman, No cry" by Bob Marley. Chord progression is: C – G – Am – F
2. "Twist and Shout" by The Beatles. Chord progression: C – F – G – C
3. "Horse with No Name". Chord progression: C – Em – D6 – Dmaj9
4. "Hey Soul Sister" by Train: Chord progression: C – G – Am – F
5. "Brown Eyed Girl" by Van Morrison. Chord progression: C – G – Am – F
6. "I won't back down" by Tom Petty. Chord progression: C – G – Am – F
7. "I am yours" by Jason Mraz. Chord progression: C – G – Am – F
8. "Let it Be" by The Beatles: C – G – Am – F
9. "With or Without You" by U2. Chord Progresion: C – G – Am – F
10. "What I Got" by Sublime. Chord progression: C – G – Am – F

You are advised to download the song above, listen to them, follow the chord progression on each to score the song. By the time you are done scoring these songs, you should have mastered C major Chord perfectly. Note that this chord progressions are approximations, the actual chord progressions may vary depending on specific arrangement or cover version you download.

D Flat Major Chord

D flat major chord which is written as Db is a triad consisting of three notes: Db (the root), F (major third), and Ab (the perfect fifth). This chord contributes very well to classical and contemporary music more amongst all others where you can find it.

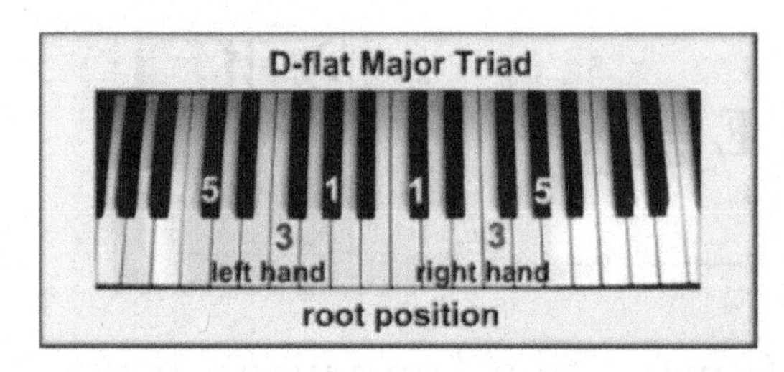

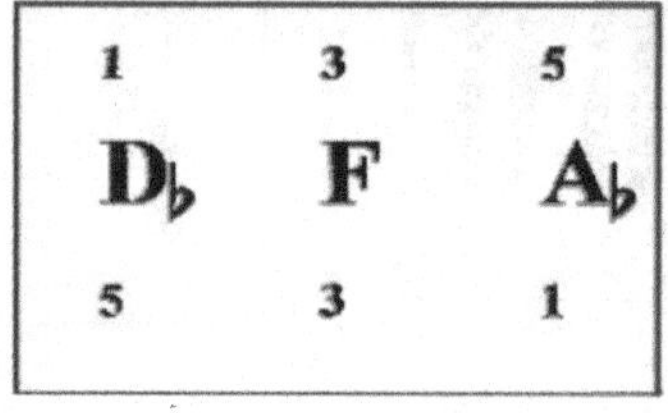

The above images are pictorial representations of D-flat (Db) major chord on a piano, musical hat, and music sheet. Examples of popular songs that were composed on Db Major Chord.

1. "Sky Fall" by Adele. Chord progression: Db – Ab – Bbm – Gb.
2. "Grenade" by Bruno Mars. Chord progression: Db – Ab – Bbm – Gb.
3. "Stay With Me" by Sam Smith. Chord progression: Db – Ab – Bbm – Gb.
4. "All of me" by John Legend. Chord progression: Db – Ab – Bbm – Gb.
5. "Counting Stars" by OneRepublic. Chord progression: Db – Ab – Bbm – Gb.
6. "Chandelier" by Sia. Chord progression: Db – Ab – Bbm – Gb.
7. "Take a bow" by Rihannah. Chord progression: Db – Bbm – Ab – Gb.
8. "Halo" by Beyonce. Chord progression: Db – Ab – Bbm – Gb.
9. "Bleeding Love" by Leona Lewis. Chord progression: Db – Ab – Bbm – Gb
10. "Un-break My Heart" by Tony Braxton. Chord progression: Db – Bbm – Ab – Gb.

You are advised to download the song above, listen to them, follow the chord progression on each to score the song. By the time you are done scoring these songs, you should have mastered D-flat major Chord perfectly. Note that this chord progressions are approximations, the actual chord progressions may vary depending on specific arrangement or cover version you download.

D Major Chord

This chord comprises three notes. These notes are: D (the root note), F# (major third), and A (the perfect fifth). This chord is widely used in composition and improvisation. The D major triad is a fundamental chord in music.

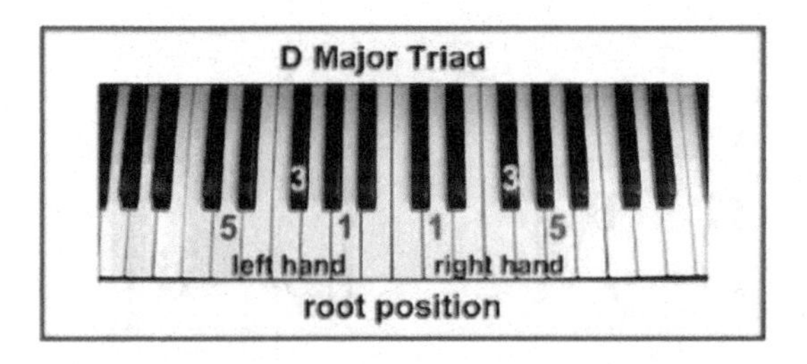

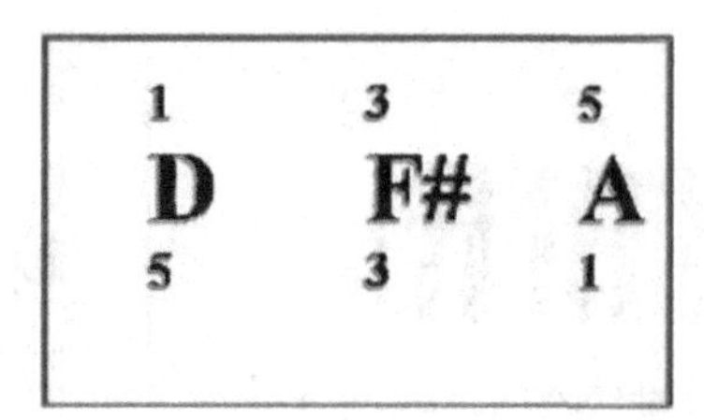

The above images are pictorial representations of D Major chord on a piano, musical chat, and music sheet. Examples of popular songs that were composed on D Major Chord are:

1. "Ho Hey" by the Lumineers. Chord progression: D – A – Bm – G
2. "Ring of Fire" by Johnny Cash. Chord progression: G – C – D
3. "I Walk the Line" by Johnny Cash. Chord progression: D – A – E – A
4. "Sweet Home Alabama" by Lynyrd Skynyrd
5. "Every Breath You Take" by The Police. Chord progression: G – Em – C – D
6. "The Gambler" by Kenny Rogers. Chord progression: G – Em – C – D
7. "Jolene" by Dolly Parton. Chord progression: C – G – D – Em – C
8. "Wonderwall" by Oasis. Chord progression: D – A – Em – G
9. "Hotel California" by Eagles. Chord progression: Bm – F# - A – E – G – D – Em
10. "Free Falling" by Tom Petty. Chord progression: D – G – A

You are advised to download the song above, listen to them, follow the chord progression on each to score the song. By the time you are done scoring these songs, you should have mastered D major Chord perfectly. Note that this chord progressions are approximations, the actual chord progressions may vary depending on specific arrangement or cover version you download.

E Flat Major Chord

E flat major chord is often written as Eb. It is a triad consisting of three notes: Eb (root note), G (the major third), and Bb (the perfect fifth). It is widely used for compositions across genres. It exemplifies harmonies that are rich and unique. The sound of it offers platform for melodic expressions and tonal exploration.

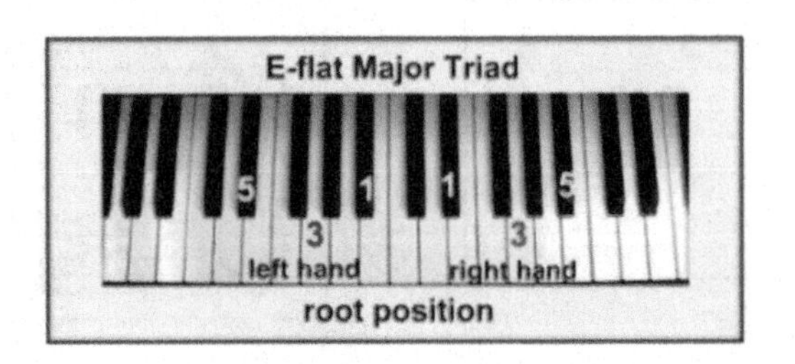

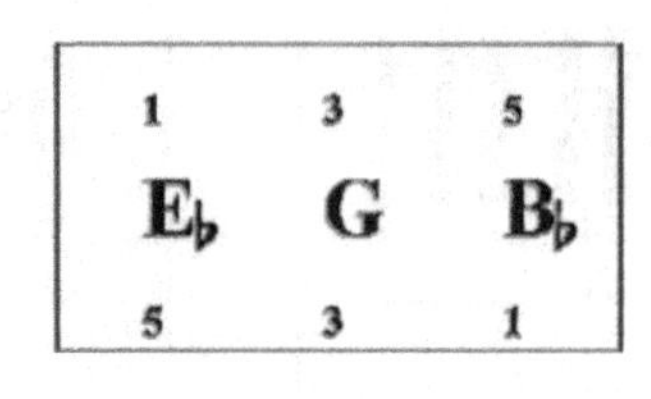

The above images are pictorial representations of E-flat Major chord on piano, musical chat, and music sheet. Examples of popular songs that were composed on E-flat Major Chord are:

1. "Rolling in The Deep" by Adele. Chord progression: Cm – Eb – Bb – Ab
2. "Chasing Pavement" by Adele. Chord progression: Eb – Bb – Fm – Ab
3. "Can't Help Falling in Love" by Elvis Presley. Chord progression: Cm – Gm – Eb – Bb
4. "Falling" by Alicia Keys. Chord progression: Eb – Ab – Bb – Cm
5. "Perfect" by Ed Sheeran. Chord progression: Gm – Eb – Bb – F
6. "Hallelujah" by Leonard Cohen. Chord progression: Eb – Bb – Cm – Ab
7. "I Will Always Love You" by Whitney Houston. Chord progression: Bb – Eb – Fm – Bb
8. "Say Something" by A Great Big World & Christina Aguilera. Chord progression: Eb – Cm – Ab – Bb
9. "Let It Go" from Frozen. Chord progression: Eb – Ab – Bb – Cm
10. "Empire State of Mind" by Jay-Z ft. Alicia Keys. Chord progression: Fm – Ab – Eb – Bb

You are advised to download the song above, listen to them, follow the chord progression on each to score the song. By the time you are done scoring these songs, you should have mastered E-flat major Chord perfectly. Note that this chord progressions are approximations, the actual chord progressions may vary depending on specific arrangement or cover version you download.

E Major Chord

E major chord is one of the fundamental chords in music. It has three notes (triad) which are: E (the root note), G# (the major third), and B (perfect fifth). It is known for its uplifting and vibrant sound that evoke joy and liveness. E major chord add brightness and energy to music composition.

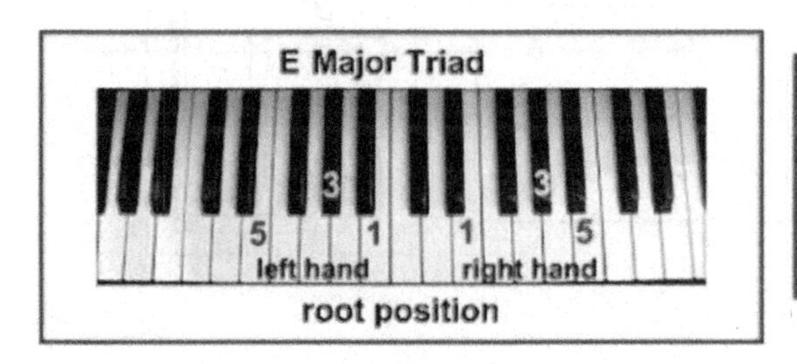

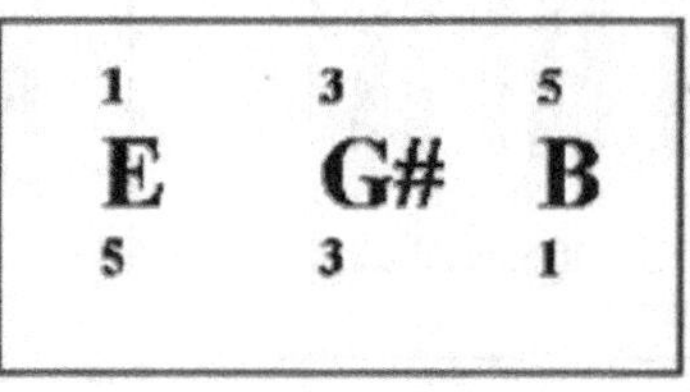

The above images are pictorial representations of E Major chord on piano, musical chat, and music sheet. Examples of popular songs that were composed on E Major Chord are:

1. "Viva La Vida" by Coldplay. Chord progression: C#m – A – E – B
2. The Lazy Song" by Bruno Mars. Chord progression: E - G#m – A – B
3. "Can't Stop the Feeling!" by Justin Timberlake. Chord progression: E – C#m – A – B
4. "Stand by Me" by Ben E King. Chord progression: E – B – C#m – A
5. "Shape of You" by Ed Sheeran. Chord progression: E – B – C#m – A
6. "Sweet Caroline" by Neil Diamond. Chord progression: E – A – D – A
7. "Take it Easy" by Eagles. Chord progression: E – G#m – A – E – B – C#m – A – E
8. "Sweet Child o' Mine" by Guns N' Roses. Chord progression: E – B – C#m – A
9. "Bad Romance" by Lady Gaga. Chord progression: Em – C – G – D – E
10. "Castle on the Hill" by Ed Sheeran. Chord progression: E – B – C#m – A

You are advised to download the song above, listen to them, follow the chord progression on each to score the song. By the time you are done scoring these songs, you should have mastered E major Chord perfectly. Note that this chord progressions are approximations, the actual chord progressions may vary depending on specific arrangement or cover version you download.

F Major Chord

F major chord is one of the cornerstones of musical harmony. It consists of three essential notes: F (the root note), A (the major third), and C (the perfect fifth). It has warm and bright tone that made it widely used in various genres.

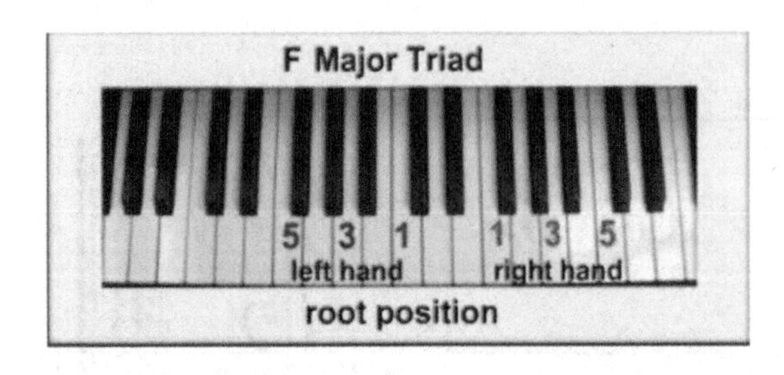

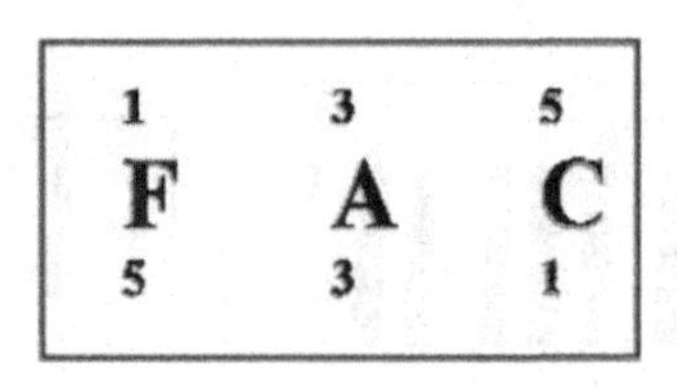

The above images are pictorial representations of F Major chord on piano, musical chat, and music sheet. Examples of popular songs that were composed on F Major Chord are:

1. Boulevard of Broken Dream" by Green Day. Chord progression: F – Am – Bb – C
2. "All Star" by Smash Mouth. Chord progression: F – G – Am – F
3. "Fireflies" by Owl City. Chord progression: F – C- Dm – Bb
4. "Riptide" by Vance Joy. Chord progression: Am – G – C – F
5. "Radioactive" by Imagine Dragon. Chord progression: Bb – F – C – Dm
6. "A Thousand Years" by Christina Perri. Chord progression: Bb – F – Gm – Eb
7. "Wagon Wheel" by Old Crow Medicine Show. Chord progression: F – C – Dm – Bb
8. "Count on Me" by Bruno Mars. Chord progression: F – Am – Dm – Bb
9. "Senorita" by Shawn Mendes & Camila Cabello. Chord progression: F – Am – Dm – Bb
10. "Take Me to Church" by Hozier. Chord progression: Am – G – F – Am

You are advised to download the songs above, listen to them, follow the chord progression on each to score the song. By the time you are done scoring these songs, you should have mastered F Major Chord perfectly. Note that this chord progressions are approximations, the actual chord progressions may vary depending on specific arrangement or cover version you download.

F Sharp/G Flat Major Chorajor Chord

This is an expressive and vibrant chord that is built as triad on three notes, i.e., F# (the root note), A# (the third major), and C# (the perfect fifth). It is one of the fundamental chords in music known as happy chord. It contributes to harmonic and melodic structures.

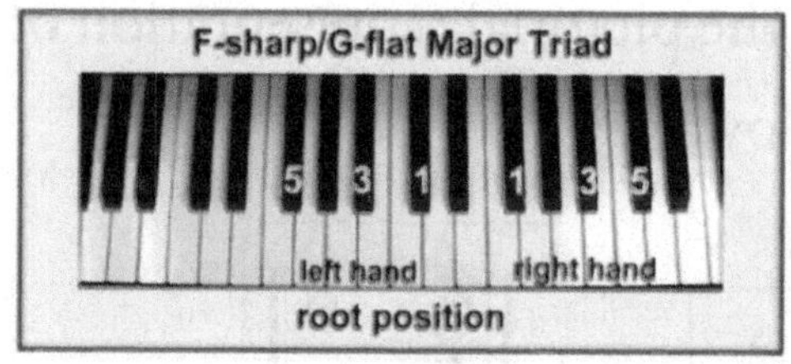

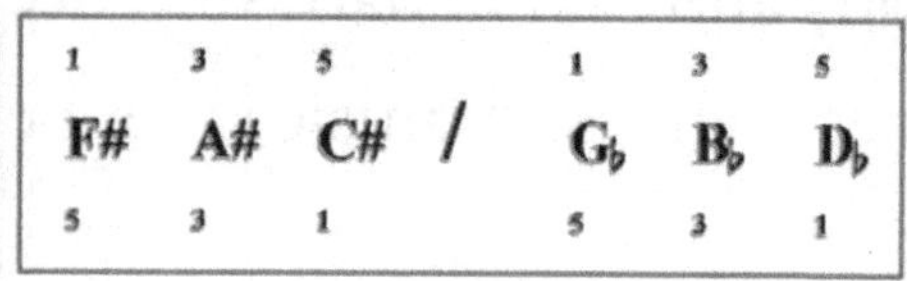

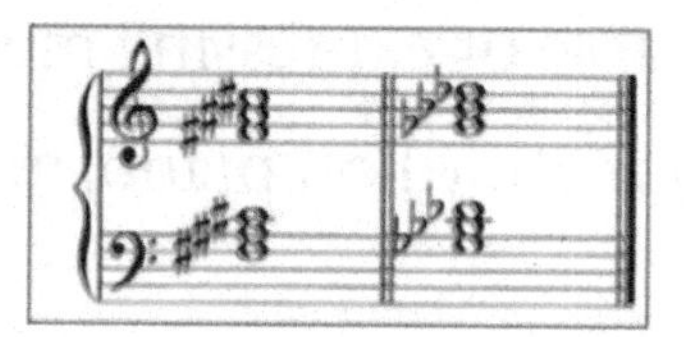

The above images are pictorial representations of F Sharp or G-flat Major chord on piano, musical chat, and music sheet. Examples of popular songs that were composed on F#/Gb Major Chord are:

1. "Love Story" by Taylor Swift. Chord progression: G#m – E – F# - C#m
2. "Thinking Out Loud" by Ed Sheeran. Chord progression: F# - B – G#m – E
3. "Rolling in the Deep" by Adele. Chord progression: C#m – E – F# – B
4. "Wrecking Ball" by Miley Cyrus. Chord progression: F#m – D#m – E – B
5. "Don't Let Me Down" by The Chainsmokers Ft Daya. Chord progression: F#m – C#m – A – E
6. "Titanum" by David Guetta ft Sia. Chord progression: F#m – D#m – E – B
7. "Sugar" by Maroon 5. Chord progression: F#m - C#m – E – B
8. "Lost Boy" by Ruth B. Chord progression: G#m – F#m – B – E
9. "See You Again" by Wiz Khalifa ft Charlie Puth. Chord progression: G#m – E – F#m – C#m
10. "Perfect" by Ed Sheeran. Chord progression: G#m – E – F#m – C#m

You are advised to download the song above, listen to them, follow the chord progression on each to score the song. By the time you are done scoring these songs, you should have mastered F major Chord perfectly. Note that this chord progressions are approximations, the actual chord progressions may vary depending on specific arrangement or cover version you download.

G Major Chord

The G major (triad) chord is one of the fundamental chords in music. It is versatile and known for its vibrant expression of happiness. It is a very bright and uplifting sound. As a triad, it consists three notes which are: G (the root note), B (the major third), and D (the perfect fifth). By experience and as expressed by many piano players, this chord is said to be capable of expressing melody and rich in harmony. See the pictorial representation of G major chord on piano, music chart, and music sheet below.

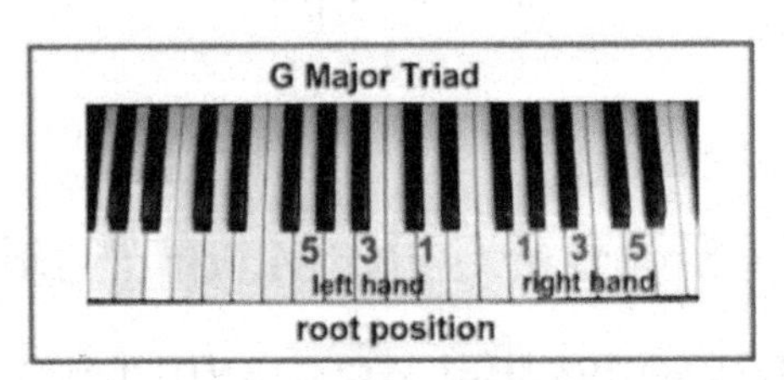

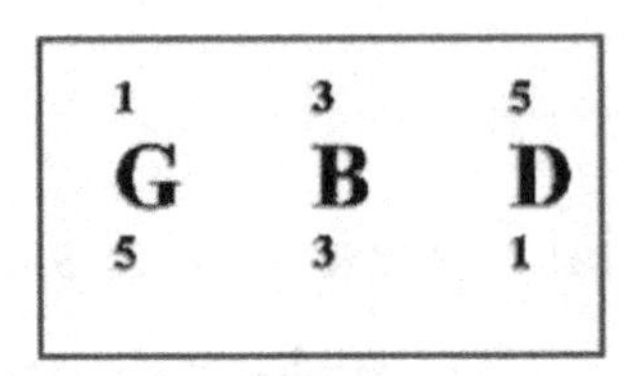

The above images are pictorial representations of G Major (triad) chord on piano, musical chat, and music sheet. Examples of popular songs that were composed on G Major Chord are:

1. "Amazed" by Lonestar. Chord progression: G – Em – C – D
2. "Temperature" by Sean Paul. Chord progression: G – Em – C -D
3. "Pride and Joy: by Stevie Ray Vaughan. Chord progression: G – C – D – G
4. "The Thrill is Gone" by B.B. King. Chord progression: G – Eb – Bb – F - Gm
5. "Dance Monkey" by Tones and I. Chord progression: G – D – Em – C
6. "Stormy Monday" by T-Bone Walker. Chord progression: G – Bm – C – G
7. "Bad Moon Rising" by Creedence Clearwater Revival. Chord progression: G – C – D – Em
8. "Highway to Hell" by AC/DC. Chord progression: G – D – C
9. "Three Little Birds" by Bob Marley. Chord progression: A – D – G
10. "Born Under a Bad Sign" by Albert King. Chord progression: G – C – D – G

You are advised to download the song above, listen to them, follow the chord progression on each to score the song. By the time you are done scoring these songs, you should have mastered G major Chord perfectly. Note that this chord progressions are approximations, the actual chord progressions may vary depending on specific arrangement or cover version you download.

A-Flat Major (Ab) Chord

The prevalence of Ab Major chord in music genres like Jazz, Classical, and Contemporary music signifies its versatility. Ab major chord is formed by combing three notes which are: Ab (the root note), C (the major third), and Eb (the perfect fifth). This sound produces very rich and bodied full tonality. See the pictorial representations of this chord below.

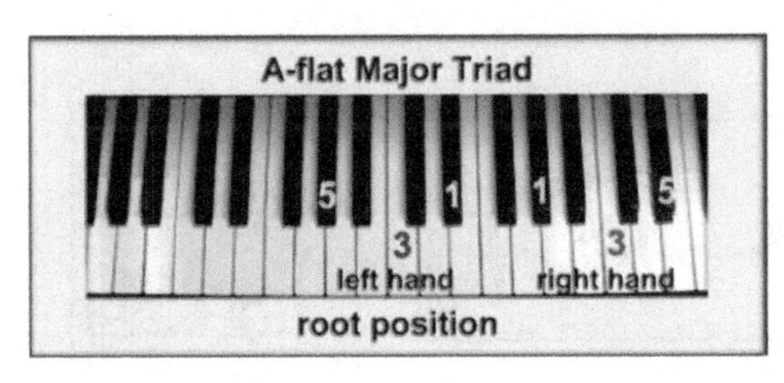

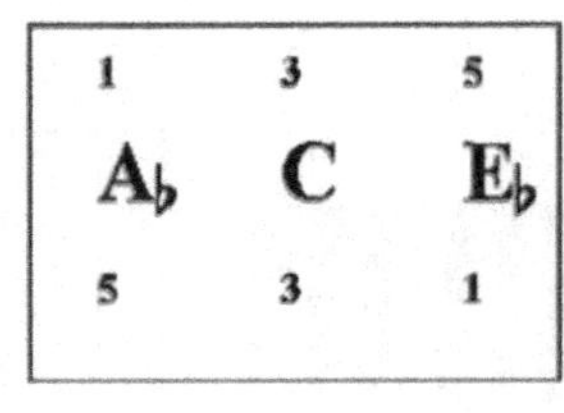

The above images are pictorial representations of A-flat Major (triad) chord on piano, musical chat, and music sheet. Examples of popular songs that have A-flat Major Chord in them with their full chord progressions are listed below.

1. "Brick House" by Commodores. Chord progression: Ab – G7 – F7 – G7
2. "Happy" by Pharrell William. Chord progression: Ab – Bbm – Gb – Db
3. "Twistin the Night Away" by Sam Cooke. Chord progression: Ab – Db – Eb
4. "La Bamba" by Ritchie Valence. Chord progression: Ab – Db – Eb
5. "Despacito" by Luis Fonsi ft. Daddy Yankee. Chord progression: Ab – Gm – Fm -Eb
6. "Roar" by Katy Perry. Chord progression: Ab – Bbm – Gm – Eb
7. "Blue Suede Shoes" by Elvis Presley. Chord progression: Ab – Db – Eb
8. Twist and Shout" by The Beatles. Chord progression: Ab – Db – Eb
9. "Get Lucky" by Daft Punk ft. Pharrell William. Chord progression: Ab – Bbm – Gm –Db
10. "Havana" by Camila Cabello ft. Young Thug. Chord progression: Ab – Gm – Fm – Eb

You are advised to download the song above, listen to them, follow the chord progression on each to score the song. By the time you are done scoring these songs, you should have mastered A-Flat Major (ab) Chord perfectly. Note that this chord progressions are approximations, the actual chord progressions may vary depending on specific arrangement or cover version you download.

A Major Chord

A major chord is one of the foundational for diverse musical expressions. It has three notes that are combined together to produce its sound. These notes are: A (the root note), C# (the major third) and E (the perfect fifth). It sounds production is that of bright and uplifting which makes it versatile across musical genres. Pictures of this chord is below for you to copy on your piano and master.

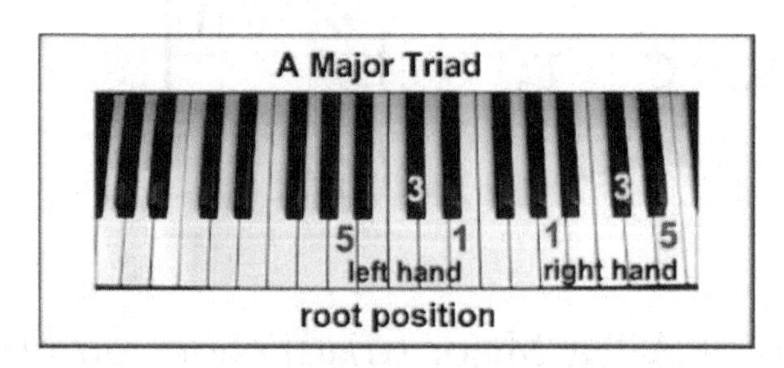

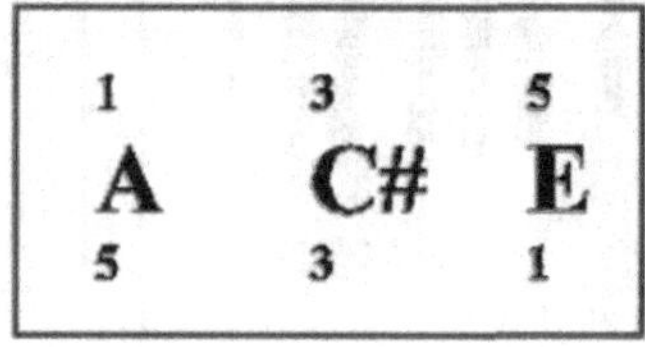

The above images are pictorial representations of A Major (triad) chord on piano, musical chat, and music sheet. Examples of popular songs that have A Major Chord in them with their full chord progressions are listed below.

1. "Sweet Home Chicago" by Robert Johnson. Chord progression: A – D – E – A
2. "Eine Klein Nachtmusik" by Wolfgang Amadeus Mozart. Chord progression: A – E – A– D – A – E – A
3. "Ain't No Sunshine" by Bill Withers. Chord progression: Am – Em – Am – Em – Am –Em – Am – E
4. "Autumn in New York" (Jazz Standard). Chord progression: A – G#m – F#m – D – Bm –E – A
5. "Before You Accuse Me" by Eric Clapton. Chord progression: A – D – A – E
6. "Moonlight Sonata" by Ludwig van Beethoven. Chord progression: Am – C – Dm – Am– E – Am
7. "Claire de Lune" by Claude Debussy. Chord progression: A – E – A – D – A – E – A
8. "Take the 'A' Train" by Duke Ellington. Chord progression: A – D9 – E7 – A
9. "Hey Jude" by The Beatles. Chord progression: A – E – F#m – D
10. "Canon in D" by Johann Pachelbel. Chord progression: D – A – Bm – F#m – G – D – A

You are advised to download the song above, listen to them, follow the chord progression on each to score the song. By the time you are done scoring these songs, you should have mastered "A" Major Chord perfectly. Note that this chord progressions are approximations, the actual chord progressions may vary depending on specific arrangement or cover version you download.

B-Flat Major

This chord is widely in use in various music genres. It contributes to both Contemporary and Classical music. It produces bright and vibrant sound. The B-flat (Bb) major composed of Bb (the root note), D (the major third), and F (perfect fifth). It has such harmonic stability and compatibility that make it one of the basic/fundamental chords for creating dynamic and soul-uplifting musical landscape. Below are the pictorial illustrations of B-flat major chord (triad).

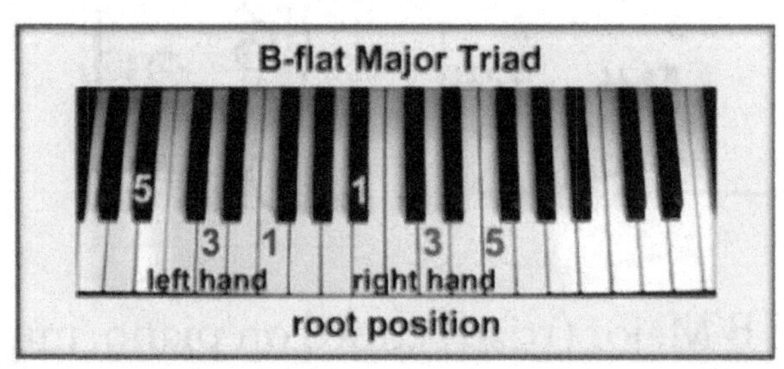

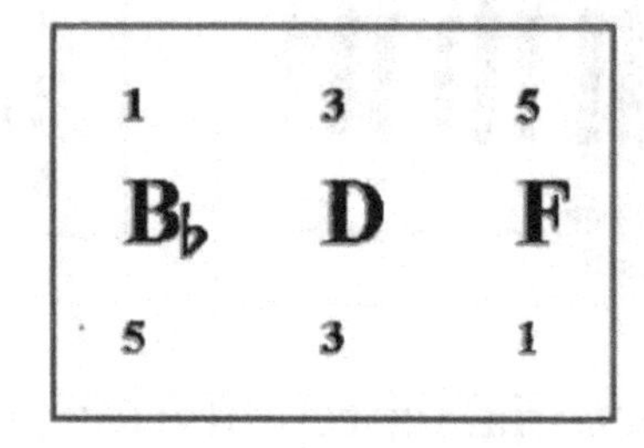

The above images are pictorial representations of B-flat Major (triad) chord on piano, musical chat, and music sheet. Examples of popular songs that have Bb Major Chord in them with their full chord progressions are listed below.

1. "Perfect" by Pink. Chord progression: Bb – Gm – Eb – F
2. "Cantaloupe Island "Herbie Hancock: Bb7 – Eb7 – Bb7 – F7
3. "Wake Me Up" by Avicii. Chord progression: Bb – F – G – E
4. "Royals" by Lorde. Chord progression: Bb – Gm – Eb – F
5. "Believer" by Imagine Dragons. Chord progression: Bb – Gm – Eb – F
6. "Fly Me to the Moon" by Frank Sinatra. Chord progression: Bb – Dm7 – Gm7 – C7
7. "All About That Bass" by Meghan Trainor. Chord progressions: Bb – F – Gm – Eb
8. "Imagine" by John Lennon. Chord progression: Bb – F – Gm – Eb
9. "Hey Jude" by The Beatles. Chord progression: Bb – F – Gm – Eb
10. "Apologize" by OneRepublic. Chord progression: Bb – F – Gm – Eb

You are advised to download the song above, listen to them, follow the chord progression on each to score the song. By the time you are done scoring these songs, you should have mastered B-flat Major Chord perfectly. Note that this chord progressions are approximations, the actual chord progressions may vary depending on specific arrangement or cover version you download.

B Major Chord

B major chord is a triad that comprised of notes B (the root note), D# (the major third), and F# (the perfect fifth). The combination of the intervals creates resonate sound and uplifting harmony. It is one of the fundamental chords that exude optimism and energy. B major chord can be leverage on in chord progressions to create dynamic and engaging harmonic sequences. The pictorial representations of this chord are shown below.

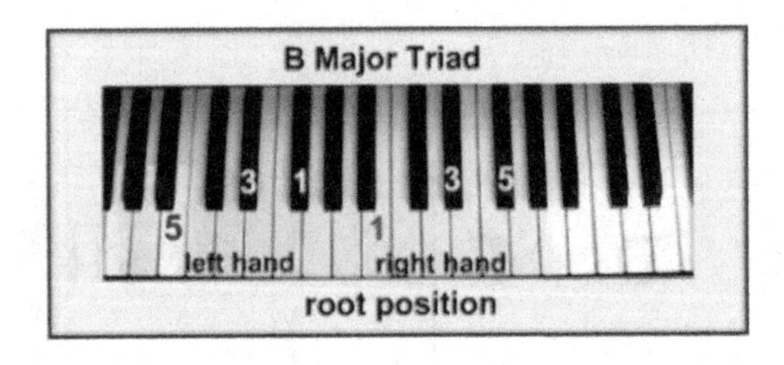

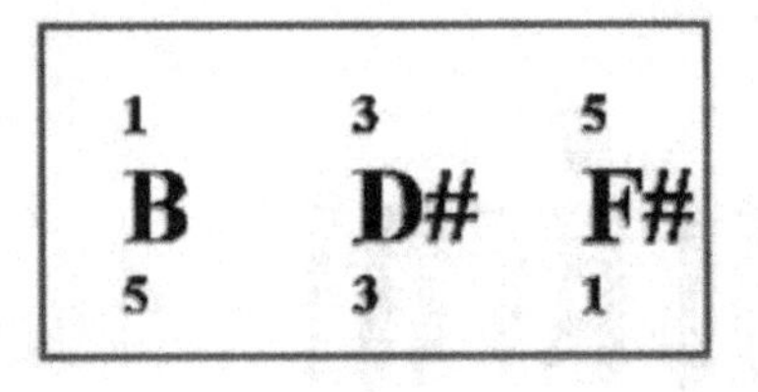

The above images are pictorial representations of B Major (triad) chord on piano, musical chat, and music sheet. Below are examples of popular songs where you can find B major chord. You are advised to score these songs to grasp this chord very well in playing it in songs of different genres and speeds.

1. "Buffalo Soldier" by Bob Marley. Chord progression: B – F# - G#m – E
2. "Could You be Loved" by Bob Marley. Chord progression: B – F# - G#m – E
3. "Skinny Love" by Bon Iver. Chord progression: B – F# - G#m – E
4. "Hotline Bling" by Drake. Chord progression: B – F# - G#m – E
5. "Sicko Mode" by Travis Scott. Chord progression: B – F# - G#m – E
6. "Electric Feel" by MGMT. Chord progression: B – F# - G#m – E
7. "Pompei" by Bastille. Chord progression: B – F# - G#m – E
8. "My Favorite Things" by John Coltrane. Chord progression: Bm – D – G – E – Bm
9. "Need You Now" by Lady A. Chord progression: B – F# - G#m – E
10. "Love Yourself" by Justin Bieber. Chord progression: B – F# - G#m – E

You are advised to download the song above, listen to them, follow the chord progression on each to score the song. By the time you are done scoring these songs, you should have mastered B Major Chord perfectly. Note that this chord progressions are approximations, the actual chord progressions may vary depending on specific arrangement or cover version you download. Also note that you may need to check explanations of other chords in the songs in this course to be able to play the full chord progressions for the suggested songs.

MINOR CHORDS (TRIAD)

The minor chord is a very close relative of a major chord, unlike the major chord, which is characterized by happiness, excitement, and energy. Minor chords sound "sad". Minor chords are built on the first, flat third, and fifth note of the major scale. The way we flat the third note is by lowering the third by a half-step. In the C minor chord, for instance, E, which is the third note in major, is lowered by a half-step to become E-flat (Eb). All the minor (triads) chords on a piano are explained below with aids of images that you should follow to understand each perfectly. The minor chords are:

C Minor Chord

The C minor chord is described as a poignant and expressive music element that belongs to the class of minor chords. It comprises three essential notes that reflect unique emotional quality. This chord is built on the root, not C, the minor third, which is Eb, and G, which is the perfect fifth. The root note C establishes a source of tonality, the minor third does the job of adding a sense of melancholia to the tone, and the perfect fifth G adds depth and stability to the tone. Below are the pictorial representations of C minor chords.

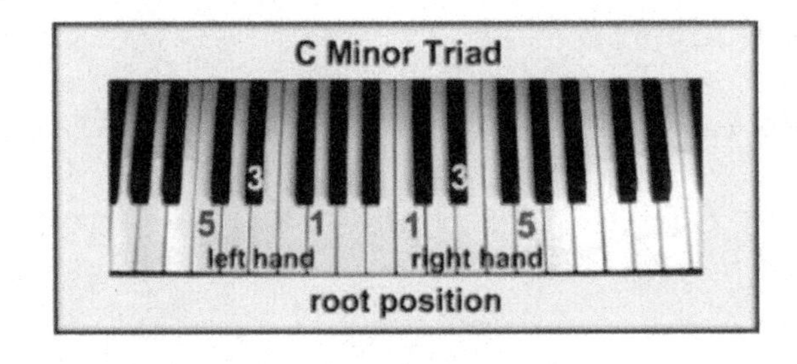

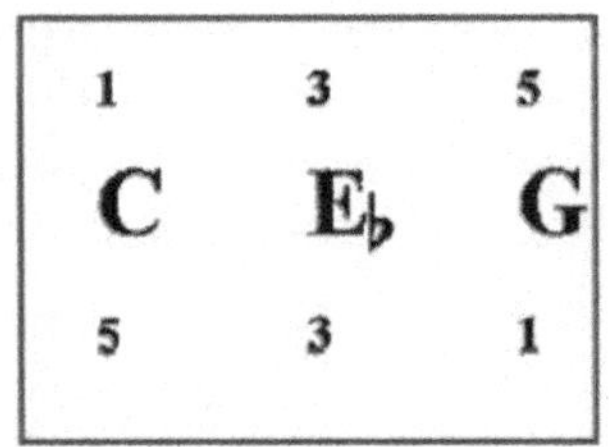

The above images are pictorial representations of C minor (triad) chords on a piano, musical chat, and music sheet. Below are examples of popular songs where you can find C minor chords. You are advised to score these songs to grasp this chord very well in playing it in songs of different genres and speeds.

1. "Shake it Out" by Florence + The Machine. Chord progression: Cm – Eb – Dm – G7
2. "Clarity" by Zedd ft. Foxes. Chord progression: Cm – Eb – Dm – G7
3. "The Times They Are a-Changin" by Bob Dylan. Chord progression: Cm – Eb – Ab – Bb
4. "I Can't Make You Love Me" by Bonnie Raitt. Chord progression: Cm – Eb – Dm – G7
5. "Use Somebody" by Kings of Leon. Chord progression: Cm – G – Ab – Bb
6. "I'd Rather Go Blind" by Etta James. Chord progression: Cm – G – Ab – Bb
7. "My Brightside" by The Killers. Chord progression: Cm – G – Ab – Bb
8. "Before He Cheats" by Carrie Underwood. Chord progression: Cm – G -Ab – F
9. "Blue Ain't Your Color" by Keith Urban. Chord progression: Cm – G – Ab – Bb
10. "Hurt" by Johnny Cash (Nine Inch Nails cover). Chord progression: C – Eb – Bb – Ab

You are advised to download the songs above, listen to them, and follow the chord progression on each to score the song. By the time you are done scoring these songs, you should have mastered C Minor Chord perfectly. Note that these chord progressions are approximations; the actual chord progressions may vary depending on the specific arrangement or cover version you download.

Also, note that you may need to check explanations of other chords in the songs in this course to be able to play the full chord progressions for the suggested songs.

C-Sharp Minor Chord (Triad)

C-sharp minor chord, which is often written as C#m, is a minor chord under a triad that consists of three notes, which are C#, E, and G#. C sharp minor chord is the relative minor of E major – it shares the same key signature with it. The minor character of this chord gives it a distinct sound compared to its major counterpart. It offers a significant contrast of mood and tonality in contrast to its major counterpart. The pictorial representations of these chords in various ways for a piano player/learner to understand are shown below.

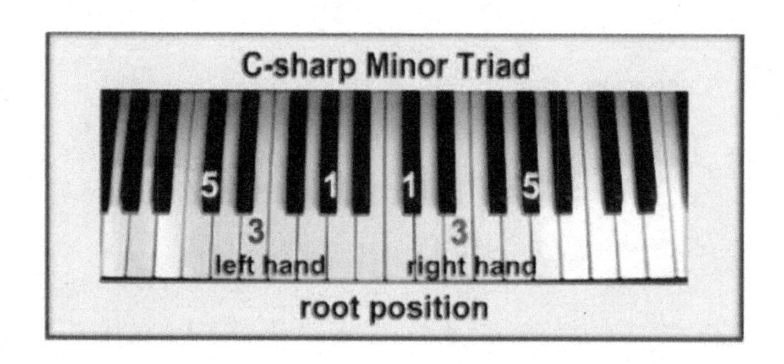

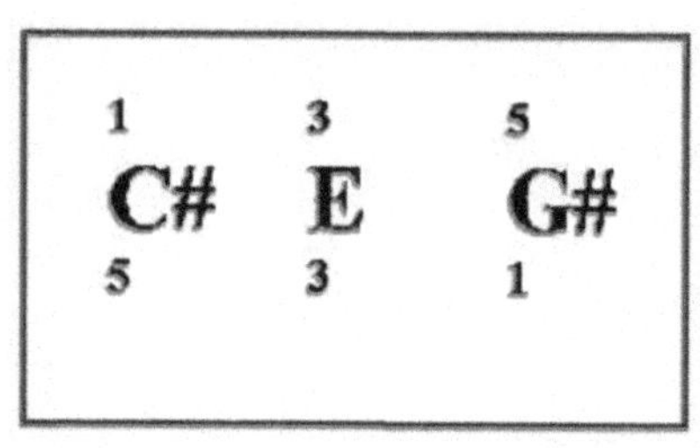

The above images are pictorial representations of C# minor (triad) chords on a piano, musical chat, and music sheet. Below are examples of popular songs where you can find C# minor chords. You are advised to score these songs to grasp this chord very well in playing it in songs of different genres and speeds.

1. "Nothing Else Matters" by Mettalica. Chord progression: C#m – E -B -A
2. "Tears in Heaven" by Eric Clapton. Chord progression: C#m – E -B -A
3. "More than Words" by Extreme. Chord progression: C#m – G#m – A – B
4. "Angie" by Rolling Stones. Chord progression: C#m – G#m – A – B
5. "Let Her Go" by Passenger. Chord progression: C#m – A – E – B
6. "Some Nights" by Fun. Chord progression: C#m – A – E – B
7. "Mad World" by Tears for Fears. Chord progression: C#m – E – A – B
8. "Bring Me to Life" by Evanescence. Chord progression: C#m – E – A – B
9. "Dust in the Wind" by Kansas. Chord progression: C#m – G – A – E
10. "A Sky Full of Stars" by Coldplay. Chord progression: C#m – E – B – A

You are advised to download the songs above, listen to them, and follow the chord progression on each to score the song. By the time you are done scoring these songs, you should have mastered them. C# Minor Chord perfectly. Note that these chord progressions are approximations; the actual chord progressions may vary depending on the specific arrangement or cover version you download. Also, note that you may need to check explanations of other chords in the songs in this course to be able to play the full chord progressions for the suggested songs.

D Minor Chord

D minor chord, which is written as DM, is a three-note chord consisting of D (the root note), F (the minor third), and A (the perfect fifth). This chord produces a sad sound, and it is usually used in various musical genres to evoke feelings of sadness, introspection, and tension. This chord is a fundamental chord in music and frequently appears in chord progressions and compositions. D minor chord is explained with pictures below.

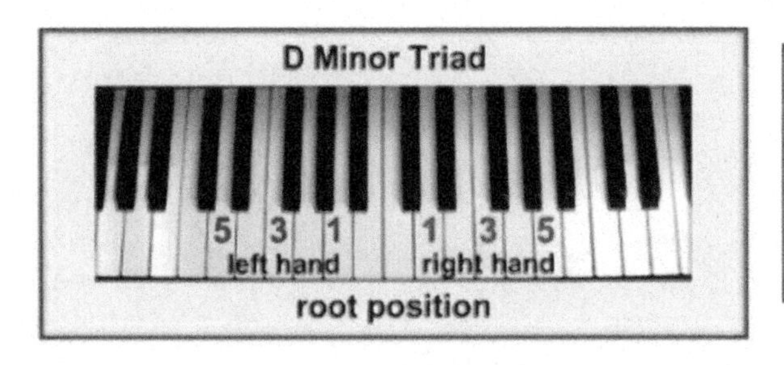

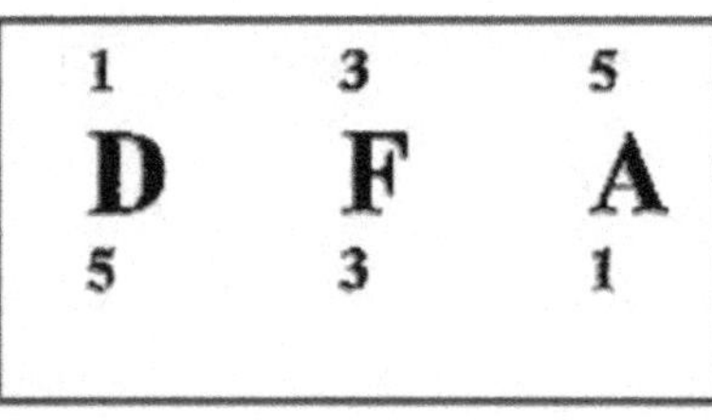

The above images are pictorial representations of D minor (triad) chords on a piano, musical chat, and music sheet. Below are examples of popular songs where you can find D minor chords. You are advised to score these songs to grasp this chord very well in playing it in songs of different genres and speeds.

1. "Zombie" by Cranberries. Chord progression: Dm – C – G – F
2. "Wicked Game" by Chris Isaak. Chord progress: Dm – C – G – F
3. "Crying" by Aerosmith. Chord progression: Dm – A – Bb – C
4. "Drive" by Incubus. Chord progression: Dm – A – Bb – C
5. "I'll Wait" by Mumford & Sons. Chord progression: Dm – F – C – G
6. "The Sound of Silence" by Simon & Garfunkel. Chord progression: Dm – Bb – F – C
7. "Dream On" by Aerosmith. Chord progression: Dm – C – G – F
8. "Unintended" by Muse. Chord progression: Dm – F – G – A
9. "All along the Watchtower" by Jimi Hendrix. Chord progression: Dm – F – G – A
10. "Creep" by Radiohead. Chord progression: Dm – F – G – C

You are advised to download the songs above, listen to them, and follow the chord progression on each to score the song. By the time you are done scoring these songs, you should have mastered the D Minor (Db) Chord perfectly. Note that these chord progressions are approximations; the actual chord progressions may vary depending on the specific arrangement or cover version you download. Also, note that you may need to check explanations of other chords in the songs in this course to be able to play the full chord progressions for the suggested songs.

D-Sharp/ E-Flat Minor Chord

D-sharp minor chord, also known as E-flat minor, is a chord that consists of three notes: D# (or Eb), F# (or GB), and A# (Bb). This chord is formed by picking three notes of D# or Eb as the root note, F# or GB as the minor third, and A# or Bb as the perfect fifth. This chord possesses the ability to promote gloom, sadness, and tension in musical compositions across various genres. It is also widely used in a variety of musical styles like jazz, pop, rock, and more. Below are the pictorial representations of the D-sharp/E-flat minor triad for you to mirror and get familiar with.

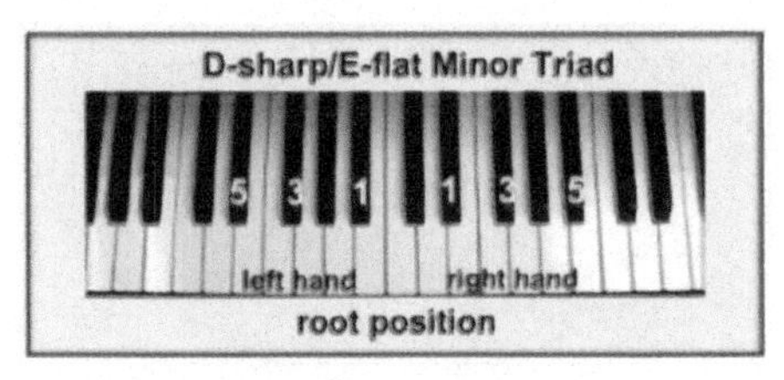

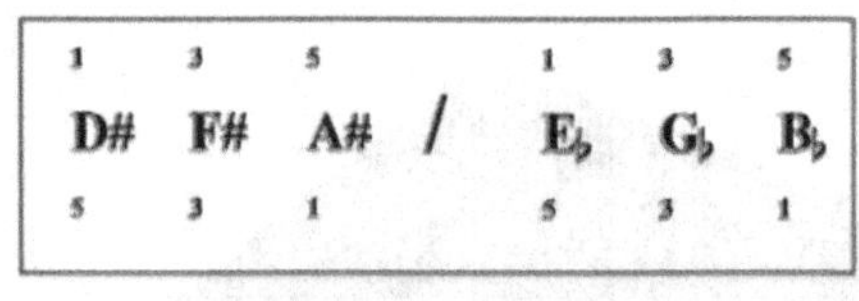

The above pictorial images are pictorial representations of the D-sharp minor triad, also known as E-flat minor, on piano, chord chat, and music sheet. You are advised to replicate the same on your piano and rehearse it for some time till you get it and get accustomed to it. Below are examples of songs that feature a D-sharp/E-flat minor chord as a main chord in their progressions.

1. "Wake Me Up When September Ends" by Green Day. Chord progression: Ebm – Gb – A– Bb
2. "Layla" by Eric Clapton. Chord progression: Ebm – D – A – E
3. "November Rain" by Guns N' Roses. Chord progression: Ebm – Gb – D – A
4. "Clocks" by Coldplay. Chord progression: Ebm – B – F# - G#
5. "Nothing Compares 2 U" by Sinead O'Connor. Chord progression: Ebm – Bb – Fb – Ab
6. "Stairway to Heaven" by Led Zeppelin. Chord progression: Ebm – Bb – Gb - Ab
7. "All I Want" by Kodaline. Chord progression: Ebm – Cb – Gb – Db
8. "Losing My Religion" by R.E.M. Chord progression: Ebm – Cb – Gb – Ab
9. "Somebody to Love" by Queen. Chord progression: Ebm – Cb – Gb – Db
10. "Everybody Hurts" by R.E.M. Chord progression: Ebm – Cb – Gb – Ab

You are advised to download the song above, listen to them, and follow the chord progression on each to score the song. By the time you are done scoring these songs, you should have mastered the D#/Eb Minor (D#/Eb) Chord perfectly. Note that these chord progressions are approximations; the actual chord progressions may vary depending on the specific arrangement or cover version you download. Also, note that you may need to check explanations of other chords in the songs in this course to be able to play the full chord progressions for the suggested songs.

E Minor Chord

An E minor chord is an emotive chord that is usually used across various genres. It comprises three notes, which are E, G, and B. E (the root note), G (the third minor), and B (the perfect fifth). It emanates a sound that is characterized as somber, melancholy, sad, and reflective, contrasting with the brightness, joy, and energy of major chords. E minor is one of the primary chords. When you're talking of harmonic progression, the E minor plays the role of adding unique harmony to progressions, adding depth and complexity to musical arrangements. Check the pictures below for E minor chords and learn them by imitating what you see on the piano, music chat, or music sheet.

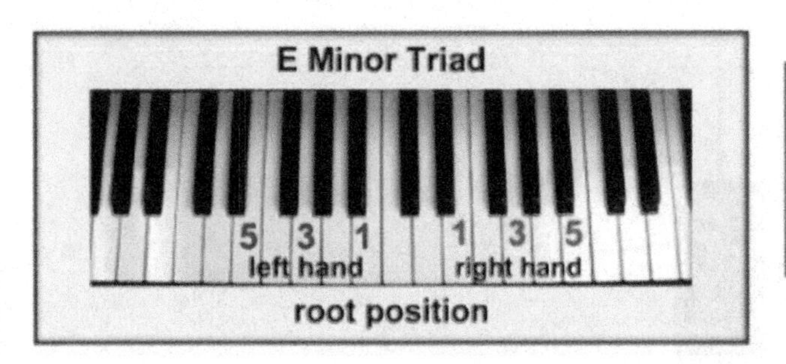

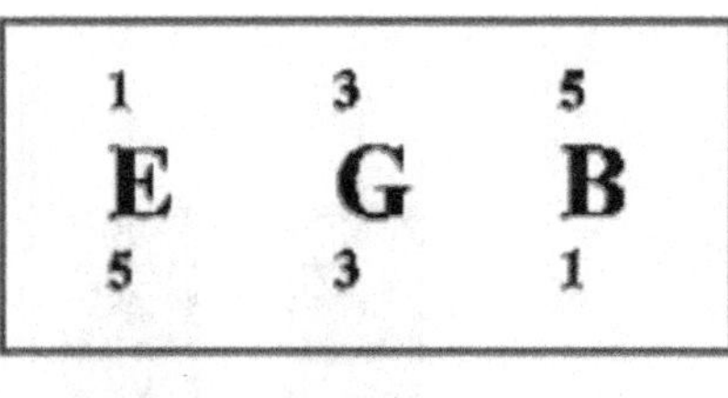

The above pictorial images are pictorial representations of E minor on piano, chord chat, and music sheet. You are advised to replicate the same on your piano and rehearse it for some time till you get it and get accustomed to it. Below are examples of songs that feature the E minor chord as a main chord in their progressions.

1. "Livin' On A Prayer" by Bon Jovi. Chord progression: Em – C – D – G
2. "Enter Sandman" by Metallica. Chord progression: Em – F – G – A
3. "When I Was Your Man" by Bruno Mars. Chord progression: Em – C – G – D
4. "Say You Won't Let Go" by James Arthur. Chord progression: Em – C – G – D
5. "Little Talks" by Of Monsters and Men. Chord progression: Em – C – G – D
6. "Budapest" by George Ezra. Chord progression: Em – C – G – D
7. "Chasing Cars" by Snow Patrol. Chord progression: Em – C – G – D
8. "Demons" by Imagine Dragon. Chord progression: Em – C – G – D
9. "I Will Follow You into the Dark" by Death Cab for Cuties. Chord progression: Em – G –D – C
10. I'm Yours" by Jason Mraz. Chord progression: Em – C – G – D

You are advised to download the songs above, listen to them, and follow the chord progression on each to score the song. By the time you are done scoring these songs, you should have mastered E Minor perfectly. Note that these chord progressions are approximations; the actual chord progressions may vary depending on the specific arrangement or cover version you download.

Also, note that you may need to check explanations of other chords in the songs in this course to be able to play the full chord progressions for the suggested songs.

F Minor Chord

The F minor chord is a fundamental component in music. It provides a very rich melancholic sound, adding depth and emotion to musical compositions across genres and styles. The F minor chord is built on three notes: F (the root note), Ab (the minor third), and C (the perfect fifth). This combination produces the F minor chord that expresses sad, reflective, and melancholy tonality and feelings. This chord structure follows the pattern of a minor chord triad, which is characterized by minor chord intervals. This interval is formed in between the root note and the third note of the interval (Ab). Below are the pictorial representations of the F minor chord.

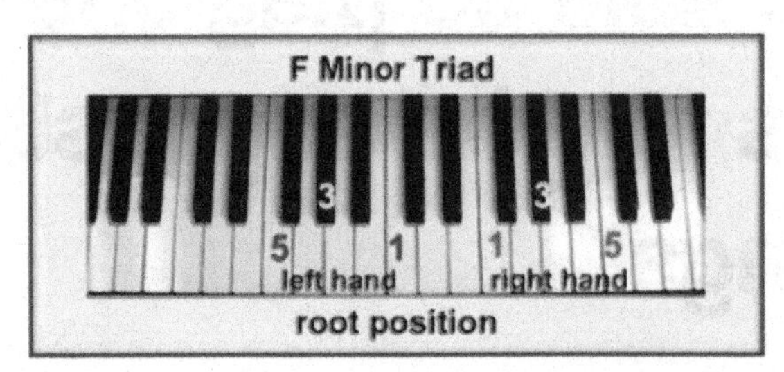

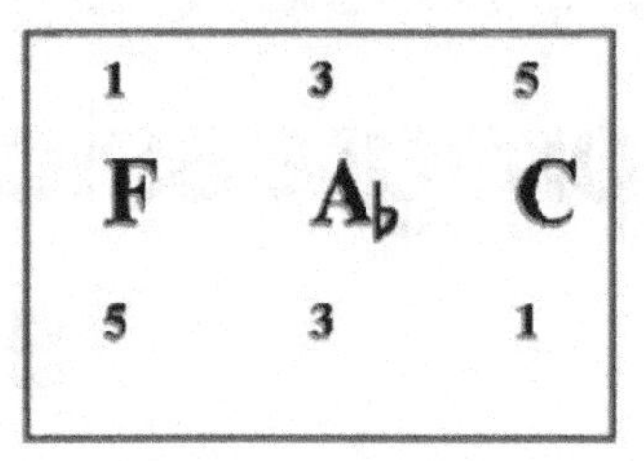

The above pictorial images are pictorial representation of F minor on piano, chord chat, and music sheet. You are advised to replicate the same on your piano and rehearse it for some time till you get it and get accustomed to it. Below are examples of songs that feature the F minor chord as a main chord in their progressions.

1. "Bohemian Rhapsody" by Queen. Chord progression: C7 – Fm – Ab – Bb – Bbm – Eb –F7
2. "Black" by Pearl Jam. Chord progression: Fm – Ab – Db – Bb
3. "Unfaithful" by Rihanna. Chord progression: Fm – Ab – Bb – Bbm – Eb
4. "She Will Be Loved" by Maroon 5. Chord progression: Fm – Ab – Bb – Eb
5. "Drops of Jupiter" by Train. Chord progression: Fm – Ab – Eb – Db
6. "How to Save a Life" by The Fray. Chord progression: Fm – Ab – Bb – Db
7. "Let it Go" by James Bay. Chord progression: Fm – Ab – Bb – Db
8. "Lost on You" by L.P. Chord progression: Fm – Ab – Db -Eb
9. "Sorry" by Justin Bieber. Chord progression: Fm – Ab – Bbm – Eb
10. "Goodbye My Lover" by James Blunt. Chord progression: Fm – Ab – Eb – Db

You are advised to download the songs above, listen to them, and follow the chord progression on each to score the song. By the time you are done scoring these songs, you should have mastered F Minor perfectly. Note that these chord progressions are approximations; the actual chord progressions may vary depending on the specific arrangement or cover version you download.

Also, note that you may need to check explanations of other chords in the songs in this course to be able to play the full chord progressions for the suggested songs.

F-Sharp Minor Chord

F-sharp minor chord like other minor triads is characterized by somber and introspective emotions. It is formed by three notes (as a triad), which are F# (the root note), A (the minor third interval), and C# (the perfect fifth). As a minor chord it evokes feelings of melancholy, a kind of longing, and introspection as against the major chords known for feelings of excitement and cheer energy.

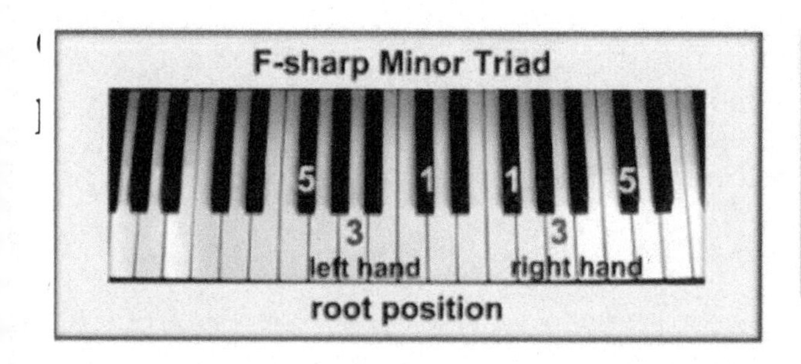

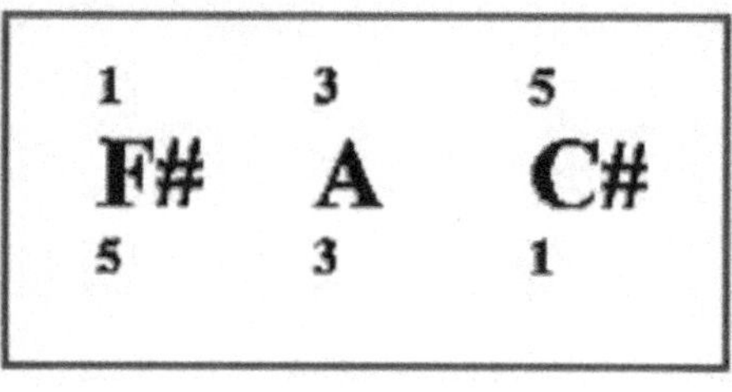

The above pictorial images are pictorial representations of F-sharp minor on piano, chord chat, and music sheet. Replicate the same on your piano and rehearse it for some time till you get it and get accustomed to it. Below are examples of songs that feature an F-sharp minor chord as a main chord in their progressions.

1. "When I Was Your Man" by Bruno Mars. Chord progression: F#m – D – A – E
2. "I'm with You" by Avril Lavigne. Chord progression: F#m – A – E – D
3. "Iris" by Goo Goo Dolls. Chord progression: F#m – A – E – D
4. "Breakeven" by The Script. Chord progression: F#m – A – E – D
5. "Let It Go" by James Bay. Chord progression: F#m – A – E – D
6. "Gravity" by John Mayer. Chord progression: F#m – A – E – D
7. "Budapest" by George Ezra. Chord progression: F#m – A – E – D
8. "How to Save a Life" by The Fray. Chord progression: F#m – A – E – D
9. "I Will Wait" by Mumford and Sons. Chord progression: F#m – A – E – D
10. "Rolling in the Deep" by Adele. Chord progression: F#m – D – A – E

You are advised to download the songs above, listen to them, and follow the chord progression on each to score the song. By the time you are done scoring these songs, you should have mastered F-sharp Minor ((F#m) perfectly. Note that these chord progressions are approximations; the actual chord progressions may vary depending on the specific arrangement or cover version you download. Also, note that you may need to check explanations of other chords in the songs in this course to be able to play the full chord progressions for the suggested songs

G Minor Chord

The G minor chord is also characterized by sad and melancholy tonality, like other minor chords that we have discussed. Its tonal quality is enclosed in emotional resonance, which makes it have a wide range of uses across many genres and styles of music. It comprises a combination of three distinct notes: G (the root note), Bb (the minor third interval), and D (the perfect fifth). One of the prominent uses of the G minor chord in music is to create a harmonic framework to elucidate and give a unique contribution to the overall mode and atmosphere. With the G minor chord, a player can successfully add complexity and depth to a musical composition and progress in a bit to evoke desired ranges of emotions from the audience. Check the diagram below to learn practically how to play the G minor chord.

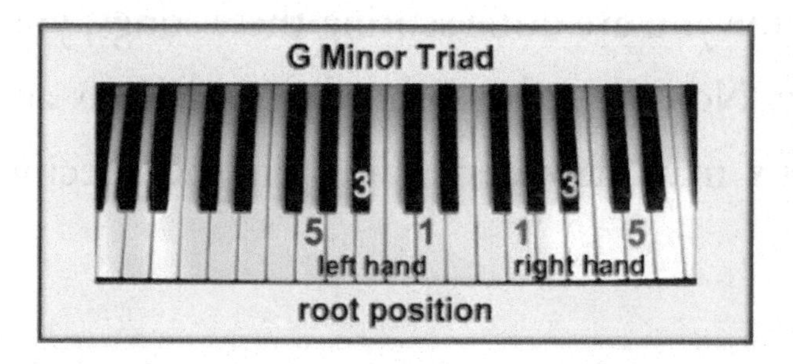

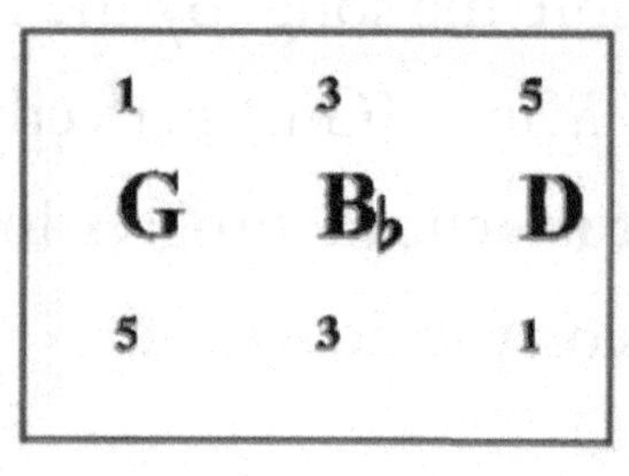

The above pictorial images are pictorial representations of G minor on piano, chord chat, and music sheet.

You are advised to replicate the same on your piano and rehearse it for some time till you get it and get accustomed to it. Below are examples of songs that feature the G minor chord as a main chord in their progressions.

1. "In the Air Tonight" by Phil Collins. Chord progression: Gm – F – C – D
2. "Boys Don't Cry" by The Cure. Chord progression: Gm – D – C – D
3. "We Are the Champion" by Queen. Chord progression: Gm – C – Gm – F – Bb – F – Gm– D – Gm
4. "I Will Survive" by Gloria Gaynor. Chord progression: Gm – Cm – D7 – Gm – Gm – Cm– D7 – Gm
5. "Zombie" by The Cranberries. Chord progression: Gm – D – Eb – F
6. "Welcome to the Black Parade" by My Chemical Romance. Chord progression: Gm – Bb– F – D
7. "Fields of Gold" by Sting. Chord progression: Gm – D – C – D – Gm – D – C – D
8. "Paint it Black" by The Rolling Stones. Chord progression: Gm – Bb – Gm – Bb – G – D– Gb – D
9. "Black Magic Woman" by Santana. Chord progression: Gm – Dm – Gm – Dm – Gm – Dm – Gm – Dm – Gm – Ab – Bb – Ab – Gm – Dm – Gm – Dm
10. "High and Dry" by Radiohead. Chord progression: Gm – F – C – D

You are advised to download the songs above, listen to them, and follow the chord progression on each to score the song. By the time you are done scoring these songs, you should have mastered G Minor (Gm) perfectly. Note that these chord progressions are approximations; the actual chord progressions may vary depending on the specific arrangement or cover version you download.

Also, you may need to check explanations of other chords in the songs in this course to be able to play the full chord progressions for the suggested songs.

G-Sharp Minor Chord

G-sharp minor (G#m) chord is one of the fundamental chords in music. It is formed from the key of G# that has thus pitches: G#, A#, B, C#, D#, E, and F#. The G# minor triad is a combination of three notes of G# (the root note), B (minor third interval), and D# (the perfect fifth). The threenote combination produces a G# minor chord that is characterized as being somber and introspective, which are the main expression of the third minor interval in the combination. Below are the pictorial representations of G-sharp minor below.

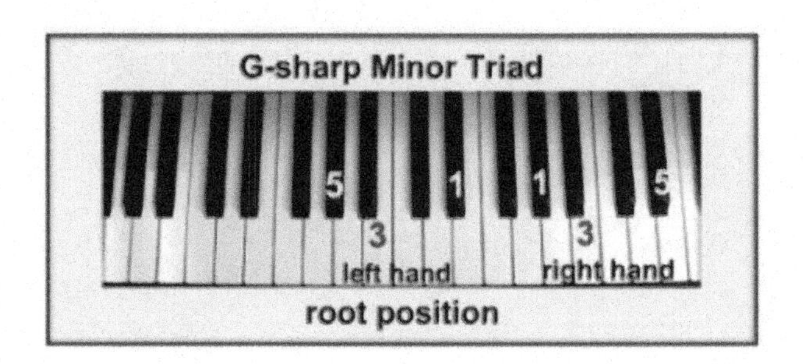

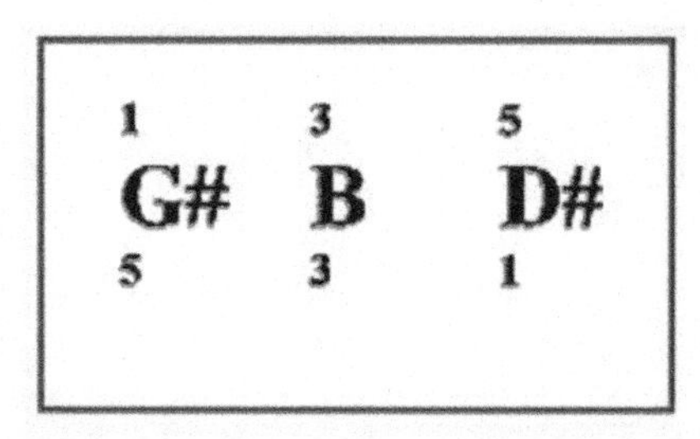

The above pictorial images are pictorial representations of G-sharp minor on piano, chord chat, and music sheet. You are advised to replicate the same on your piano and rehearse it for some time till you get it and get accustomed to it. Below are examples of songs that feature a G-sharp minor chord as a main chord in their progressions.

1. "Summertime Sadness" by Lana Del Rey. Chord progression: G#m – E – B F#
2. "Stay" by Zedd & Alessia Cara. Chord progression: G#m – E – B F#
3. "Ghost" by Ella Henderson. Chord progression: G#m – E – B F#
4. "Somebody That I Used to Know" by Gotye ft. Kimbra. Chord progression: G#m – E – B F#
5. "Stay" by Rihanna ft. Mikky Ekko. Chord progression: G#m – E – B – F#
6. "Love Song" by Sara Bareilles. Chord progression: G#m – E – B – F#
7. "Every Rose Has Its Thorn" by Poison. Chord progression: G#m – E – B – F#
8. "Mr. Brightside" by The Killers. G#m – E – F# - B
9. "Bitter Sweet Symphony" by The Verve. Chord progression: G#m – F# - E – B
10. "Teenage Dream" by Katy Perry. Chord progression: G#m – E – B – F#

You are advised to download the songs above, listen to them, and follow the chord progression on each to score the song. By the time you are done scoring these songs, you should have mastered G-sharp minor (G#m) perfectly. Note that these chord progressions are approximations; the actual chord progressions may vary depending on the specific arrangement or cover version you download.

Also, note that you may need to check explanations of other chords in the songs in this course to be able to play the full chord progressions for the suggested songs.

A Minor Chord

This minor chord (Am) is built from the key of A. The key of A has A, B, C, D, E, F, and G as its pitches. A minor chord is formed with three notes: A (the root note), C (the minor third interval), and E (the perfect fifth). The combination produces a minor triad that is rich in emotive expressions. This chord is often implored in a piece or chord progression of songs to create tension before resolving to other chords within the key. Study the diagrams below to master the playing of a minor chord on your keyboard, music chat, and music sheet.

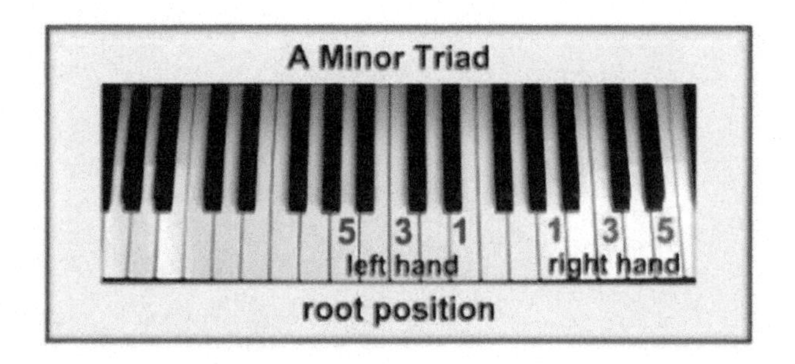

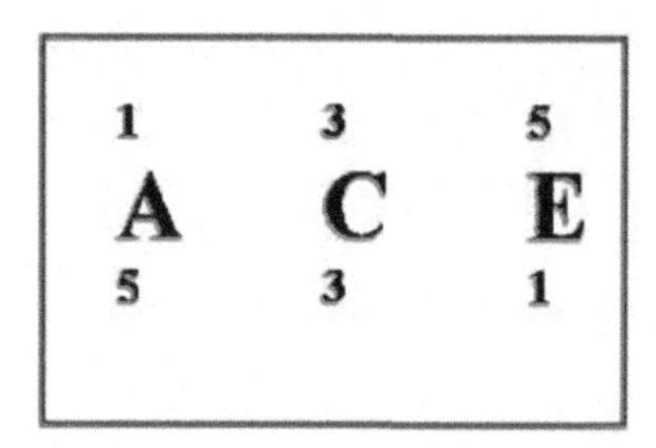

The above pictorial images are pictorial representations of A minor on piano, chord chat, and music sheet. You are advised to replicate the same on your piano and rehearse it for some time till you get it and get accustomed to it. Below are examples of songs that feature A minor chord as a main chord in their progressions.

1. "All of Me" by Billie Holiday. Chord progression: Am – Dm – E7 – Am
2. "Use Somebody" by Kings of Leon. Chord progression: Am – F – C – G
3. "Zombie" by Bad Wolves. Chord progression: Am – F – C – G
4. "Hallelujah" by Jeff Buckley. Chord progression: Am – F – G – Em
5. "High Hopes" by Panic! At The Disco. Chord progression: Am – C – F – G
6. "Wonderful Tonight" by Eric Clapton. Chord progression: Am – D – F – G
7. "Fast Car" by Tracy Chapman. Am – G – C – D
8. "Don't Speak" by No Doubt. Chord progression: Am – F – C – G
9. "Under the Bridge" by Red Hot Chili Pepper. Chord progression: Am – F – C – G
10. "Let It Be" by The Beatles. Chord progression: Am – G – F – C

Download the songs above, listen to them, and follow the chord progressions on each to score the songs. By the time you are done scoring these songs, you should have mastered A minor (Am) perfectly.

Note that these chord progressions are approximations; the actual chord progressions may vary depending on the specific arrangement or cover version you download. Also, note that you may need to check explanations of other chords in the songs in this course to be able to play the full chord progressions for the suggested songs.

B-Flat Minor Chord

A B-flat minor chord is a minor chord that is produced from three notes of B-flat, D-flat, and F. B-flat minor chord is formed from B-flat minor scale, which consists of notes B-flat, C, D-flat, E-flat, F, G-flat, and A-flat. The B-flat (triad) chord consists of B-flat as the root note, D-flat as the minor third interval, and F note as the perfect fifth. The combination of these three notes produces the B-flat chord. Like other minor chords, the D-flat in this chord defines the chord's minor quality that creates the minor chords' somber and melancholic expressions. Below are diagrams for you to follow to be able to play this chord effortlessly

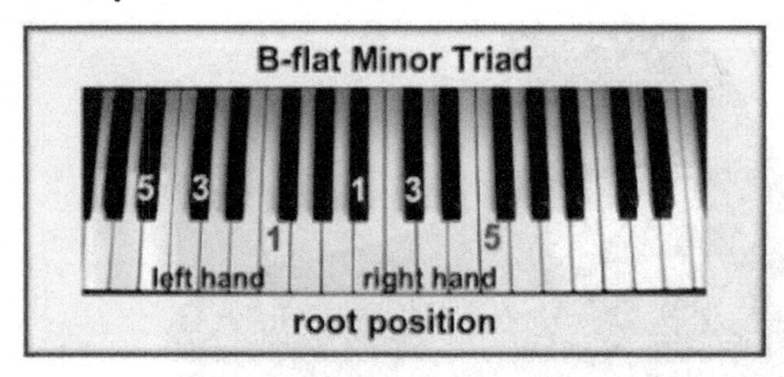

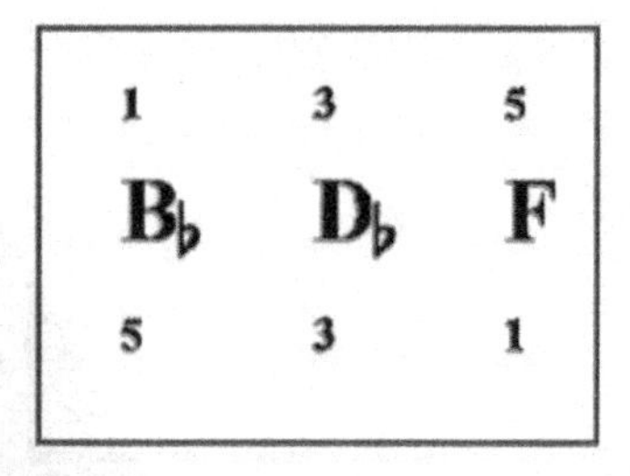

The above pictorial images are pictorial representations of B-flat minor on piano, chord chat, and music sheet. You are advised to replicate the same on your piano and rehearse it for some time till you get it and get accustomed to it. Below are examples of songs that feature a B-flat minor chord as a main chord in their progressions.

1. "Space Oddity" by David Bowie. Chord progression: Bbm – F# - G# - E
2. "Mad World" by Gary Jules. Chord progression: Bbm – Gb - Db – Ab
3. "I Miss You" by Blinks-182. Chord progression: Bbm – F# - G# - E
4. "The Power of Love" by Celine Dion. Chord progression: Bbm – F# - G# - E
5. "Cry Me a River" by Justin Timberlake. Chord progression: Bbm – Gb - Db – Ab
6. "Rise Up" by Andra Day. Chord progression: Bbm – Gb - Db – Ab
7. "The Night We Met" by Lord Huron. Chord progression: Bbm – Gb - Db – Ab
8. "Bother" by Stone Sour. Chord progression: Bbm – F - Db – Ab
9. "Stitches" by Shawn Mendes. Chord progression: Bbm – Gb - Db – Ab
10. "Eleanor Rigby" by The Beatles. Chord progression: Bbm – Gb - Db – Ab

You are advised to download the songs above, listen to them, and follow the chord progression on each to score the songs. By the time you are done scoring these songs, you should have mastered B-flat minor (Bbm) perfectly.

Note that these chord progressions are approximations; the actual chord progressions may vary depending on the specific arrangement or cover version you download. Also, note that you may need to check explanations of other chords in the songs in this course to be able to play the full chord progressions for the suggested songs.

B Minor (Triad) Chord

Like other minor triads, the B minor chord is a fundamental chord consist the combination of three notes: B, D, and F. This chord is rooted and formed from the B minor scale with thus notes:

- B, C#, D, E, F#, G, and A. B note/key serves as the root note.
- D is the minor interval that conveys the dynamic feeling and melancholic introspection in this combination.
- F # serves as the perfect in this combination to form a B-minor chord.

The diagram below will guide you to play it perfectly on the keyboard.

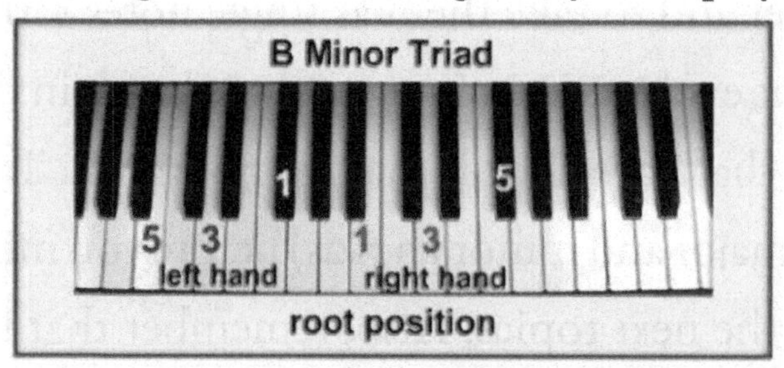

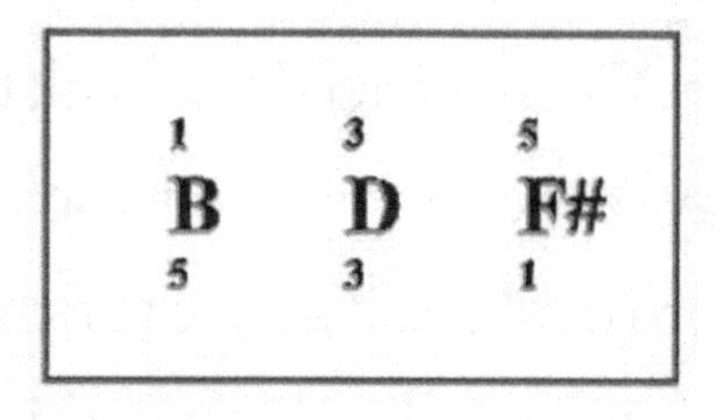

The above pictorial images are pictorial representations of B minor on piano, chord chat, and music sheet. You are advised to replicate the same on your piano and rehearse it for some time till you get it and get accustomed to it. Below are examples of songs that feature the B minor chord as a main chord in their progressions.

1. "Africa" by Toto. Chord progression: Bm – G – D – A
2. "I'm Not the Only One" by Sam Smith. Chord progression: Bm – A – G – D
3. "You Say" by Lauren Daigle. Chord progression: Bm – A – G – D
4. "Love Me Like You Do" by Ellie Goulding. Chord progression: Bm – A – G – D
5. "Sunday Morning" by Maroon 5. Chord progression: Bm – A – G – D
6. "Happier" by Marshmello ft. Bastille. Chord progression: Bm – G – D – A
7. "Shape of My Heart" by Sting. Chord progression: Bm – A – G – D
8. "Best Part" by Daniel Caesar ft. H.E.R. Chord progression: Bm – F#7 – Gmaj7 – Emaj7
9. "Stressed Out" by TwentyOne Pilots. Chord progression: Bm – A – G – D
10. "Circles" by Post Malone. Chord progression: Bm – A – G – D

You are advised to download the songs above, listen to them, and follow the chord progression on each to score the song. By the time you are done scoring these songs, you should have mastered B minor (Bm) perfectly. Note that these chord progressions are approximations; the actual chord progressions may vary depending on the specific arrangement or cover version you download.

Also, note that you may need to check explanations of other chords in the songs in this course to be able to play the full chord progressions for the suggested songs.

Note that all the alphabets in the songs presented as examples under each chord are chords and no single notes - never forget we are dealing with chords and not notes. This is a friendly reminder to avoid being confused by the alphabet and to take them as single notes rather than the chords they are. You may need to check the explanation of some other chords in this course to be able to play some songs listed above that have chords that are not triads. Take time and learn each chord explained above (both major and minor chords) before you move on to learn the complex ones to be discussed in the next topics. Also, remember that the chord progressions given for all the songs are approximations of all chords played in the song. You may need to download the music sheets or chord progressions to know how they apply to the songs, e.g. verses, choruses, and what have you in each song.

DIMINISHED CHORDS

You shouldn't be bothered by the seemingly complex terms this comes with. When we say a chord is diminished in piano playing, look at it as a minor chord that has been shrunk. The diminished chord concept is very related to the minor cord concept in the sense that the third note of the three notes combines to form a diminished chord and is also lowered by half a step, exactly like the minor third intervals of the minor chord. The only difference is that the fifth notes here are lowered by a half-step, too. In other words, a diminished chord consists of a root note, a minor third, and a diminished fifth. For example, in the key of C major, the C diminished will be C (the root note), Eb (the minor third), and Gb (the diminished fifth).

Each of the diminished chords will be discussed in very simple ways, one after the other, with the aid of diagrams and songs where such chord features will be provided for you in case you are done mastering the chords and willing to learn from actual songs.

Please relax and enjoy the journey of learning these amazing chords and applying them to create wonderful effects in your playing. Below are the diminished chords we have in music and their explanations.

C Diminished (Cdim) Chord

C diminished chord with the chord symbol of Cdim is a diminished chord that is formed by three notes, having key C as its root note, Eb as its third minor, and Gb as its diminished fifth. Like other diminished chords, C diminished chords (Cdim) are used in a musical piece to create a kind of tense and dissonance. In a piece with a functional harmonic structure, Cdim is often used as a passing chord or deployed as a dominant substitute to add a form of complexity to the progression. It is worth noting the symmetrical nature of the Cdim chord; it shares the same root with Eb diminished and Gb diminished, which makes it a very useful chord for modulation (modulation is a transition between keys within a piece of music. For instance, moving from key C to C# while playing a piece) and chromatism. Cdim is also very useful in various genres and musical styleslike jazz, pop, classical, etc., adding color, depth, and complexity to musical progressions. Below are the pictorial representations of Cdim for you to study, learn, and practice.

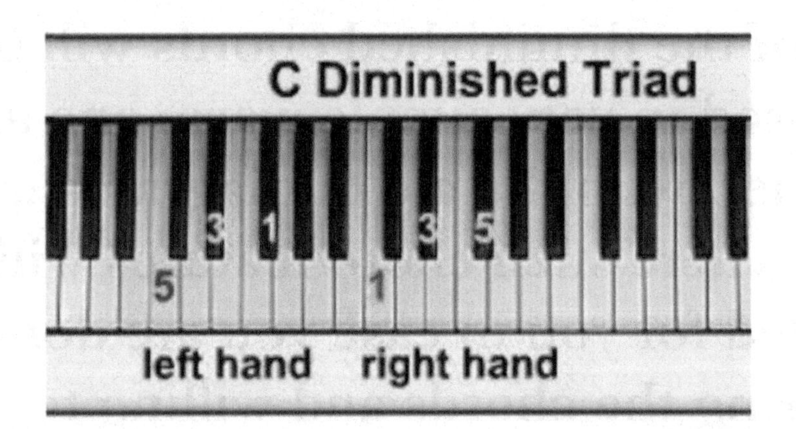

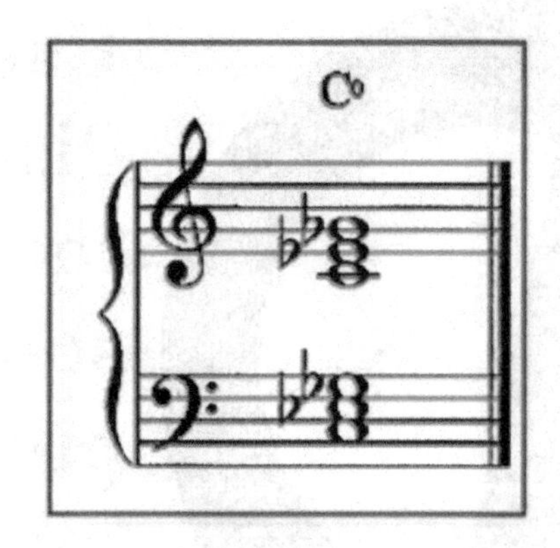

The images above represent the C-diminished piano and music sheet chords. You are advised to replicate the same on your piano and rehearse it until you get accustomed to it. Below are examples of songs that feature the C diminished chord in their progressions.

1. "S.O.S" by Abba. Chord progression: Cdim – G – Am – F
2. "Angels" by Robbie Williams. Chord progression: Cdim – G – Am – F
3. "Boogie Wonderland" by Earth, Wind & Fire. Chord progression: Cdim – G – Am – F
4. "Waterloo" by Abba. Chord progression: Cdim – G – Am – F
5. "Summer of '69" by Bryan Adams. Chord progression: Cdim – G – Am – F
6. "One Kiss" by Calvin Harris & Dua Lipa. Chord progression: Cdim – G – Am – F
7. "Don't Start Now" by Dua Lipa. Cdim – A – F – G
8. "Shivers" by Ed Sheeran. Chord progression: Cdim – G – Am – F
9. "Prayer in C" by Robin Schulz ft. Lilly Wood & The Prick. Chord progression: Cdim – G– Am – E
10. "Sweet but Psycho" by Ava Max. Chord progression: Cdim – G – Am – F

You are advised to download the songs above, listen to them, and follow the chord progression on each to score the song. By the time you are done scoring these songs, you should have mastered the C diminished chord (Cdim) perfectly. Note that these chord progressions are approximations; the actual chord progressions may vary depending on the specific arrangement or cover version you download.

Also, note that you may need to check explanations of other chords in the songs in this course to be able to play the full chord progressions for the suggested songs.

C-Sharp Dinimished Triad

C-sharp diminished chord, also known as C#dim, is a diminished triad that is formed with three notes of C#, E, and G. The C# is the root note for this chord, key E functions as the minor third, and G stands as the diminished fifth. Like other diminished chords, this chord is often used as a passing chord to realize and create tension in compositions. It is also often deployed intentionally to add complexity and intrigue to a musical composition. The C#dim also allows for easy modulation to other keys related to it. This chord can enhance the depth of emotion and harmonic progression structure as a result of its dissonant nature/character. Below are the pictorial representations of the C-sharp diminished chord.

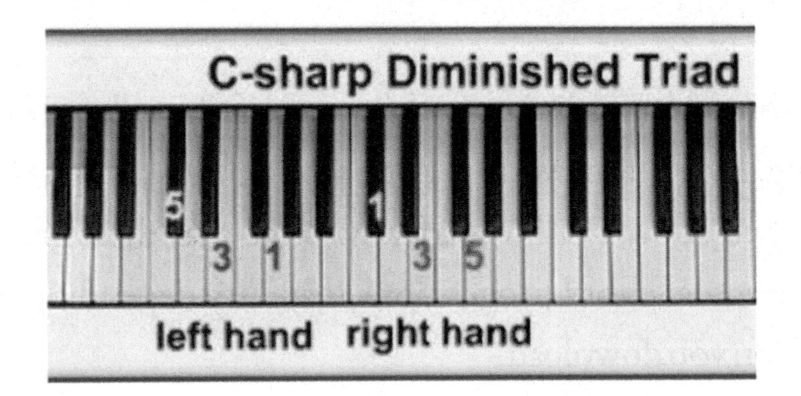

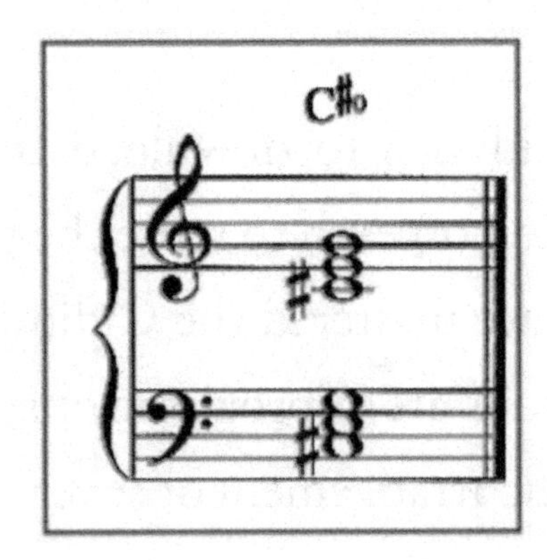

The above pictorial images are pictorial representations of C-sharp (C#dim) diminished chords on the piano and music sheets.

You are advised to replicate the same on your piano and rehearse it for some time till you get it and get accustomed to it.

Below are examples of songs that feature C-sharp diminished chords in their progressions.

1. "Star Boy" by The Weekend ft. Daft Punk. Chord progression: C#dim – A – E – F
2. "Wake Me Up" by Avicii. Chord progression: C#dim – A – E – F
3. "Mia" by Bad Bunny ft. Drake. Chord progression: C#dim – B – F#m – A
4. "Sick Boy" by The Chainsmokers. Chord progression: C#dim – E – B – F#m
5. "Truth Hurts" by Lizzo. Chord progression: C#dim – A – E – F
6. "Humble" by Kendrick Lamar. Chord progression: C#dim – A – E – F
7. "Without Me" by Halsey. Chord progression: C#dim – E – B – F#m
8. "Savage Love" by Jawsh 685 & Jason Derulo. Chord progression: C#dim – B – G#m –F#
9. "Levitating" by Dua Lipa ft. DaBay. Chord progression: C#dim – B – A#m – F#
10. "God's Plan" by Drake. Chord progression: C#dim – A – E – B

You are advised to download the songs above, listen to them, and follow the chord progression on each to score the song. By the time you are done scoring these songs, you should have mastered the C-sharp diminished chord (C#dim) perfectly. Note that these chord progressions are approximations; the actual chord progressions may vary depending on the specific arrangement or cover version you download. Also, note that you may need to check explanations of other chords in the songs in this course to be able to play the full chord progressions for the suggested songs.

D Diminished Chord

The D diminished chord with the short chord code of Ddim comprises notes D, F, and Ab. It is popularly used for two things in musical composition – one is to create suspense, and two is to transition to other related keys in the form of modulation while playing. It produces a dissonance sound that emanates from the interval of the minor third of D and F and the interval between the diminished fifth of D and Ab. A diminished chord elicit a high level of emotion in music and creates a certain complexity to such a piece or progression. Below are the pictorial representations of D diminished (Ddim).

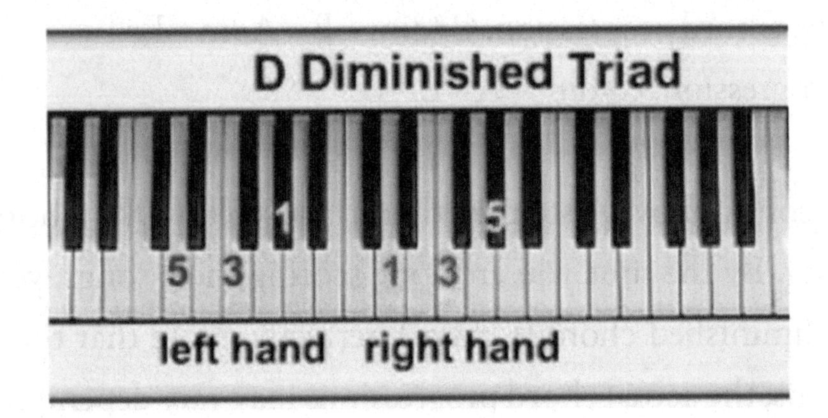

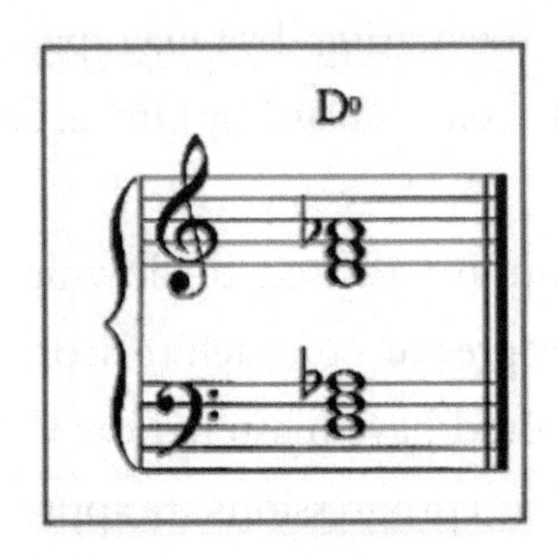

The above pictorial images are pictorial representations of D diminished (Ddim) chords on the piano and music sheet. You are advised to replicate the same on your piano and rehearse it until you get accustomed to it.

Below are examples of songs that feature D diminished chord in their progressions.

1. "Finesse" by Bruno Mars ft. Cardi B. Chord progression: Ddim – A – Bm – G
2. "Crazy in Love" by Beyonce ft. Jay Z. Chord progression: Ddim – A – Bm – G
3. "Blinding Light" by The Weekends. Chord progression: Ddim – F#m – A – E
4. "Watermelon Sugar" by Harry Styles. Chord progression: Ddim – G – A – B
5. "In My Feelings" by Drake. Chord progression: Ddim - A – Bm – G
6. "Sunflower" by Post Malone & Swae Lee. Chord progression: Ddim – A – Bm – G
7. "SICKO MODE" by Travis Scott ft. Drake. Chord progression: Ddim – A – Bm – G
8. "Good as Hell" by Lizzo. Chord progression: Ddim – A – Bm – G
9. "Love on the Brain" by Rihanna. Chord progression: Ddim – A – Bm – G
10. "Congratulations" by Post Malone ft. Quavo. Chord progression: Ddim – A – Bm – G

You are advised to download the songs above, listen to them, and follow the chord progression on each to score the song. By the time you are done scoring these songs, you should have mastered the D diminished chord (Ddim) perfectly. Note that these chord progressions are approximations; the actual chord progressions may vary depending on the specific arrangement or cover version you download.

Also, you may need to check explanations of other chords in the songs in this course to be able to play the full chord progressions for the suggested songs.

D-Sharp (D#dim) Diminished Chord

Like other diminished chords, it exudes dissonance and tense quality. It is usually used as a passing chord in functional harmonies. Its symmetrical quality makes it useful like others for modulation and nice chromatic movement. It consists of three notes, which are D#, F#, and A. The D# serves as the root note, F# is the minor third interval, and A is the diminished fifth.

Below are the pictorial representations of the D#dim chord

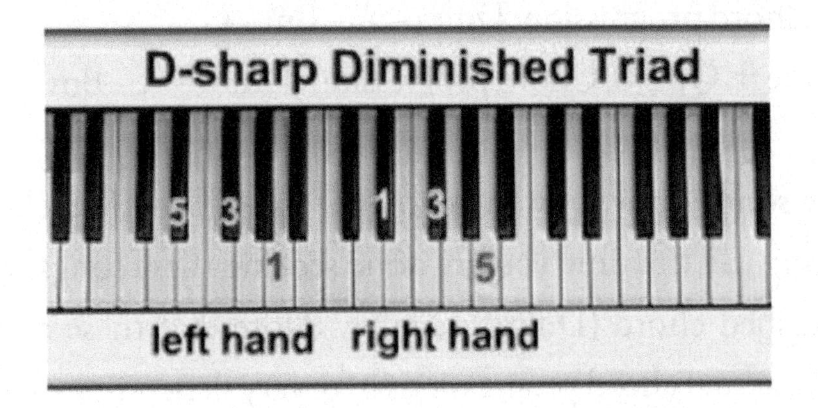

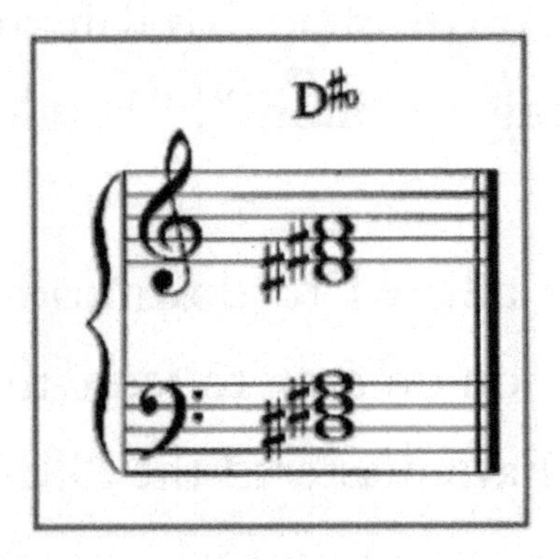

The above pictorial images are pictorial representations of D-sharp diminished (D#dim) chords on the piano and music sheet.

You are advised to replicate the same on your piano and rehearse it until you get accustomed to it.

Below are examples of songs that feature D-sharp diminished chords in their progressions.

1. "Yummy" by Justin Bieber. Chord progression: D#dim – B – C# - G#
2. "Stay" by Kid LAROI & Justin Bieber. Chord progression: D#dim – B – C# - G#
3. "Rockstar" by Post Malone. Chord progression: D#dim – B – C# - G#
4. "Butter" by BTS. Chord progression: D#dim – B – C# - G#
5. "Mood" by 24kGoldn ft. iann dior. Chord progression: D#dim – B – C# - G#
6. "Bad Guy" by Billie Eilish. Chord progression: D#dim – B – C# - G#
7. "Dance Monkey" by Tones and I. Chord progression: D#dim – B – C# - G#
8. "Sucker" by Jonas Brothers. Chord progression: D#dim – B – C# - G#
9. "Uptown Funk" by Mark Ronson ft. Bruno Mars. Chord progression: D#dim – B – C# -G#
10. "Happier" by Marshmello ft. Bastille. Chord progression: D#dim – B – C# - G#

You are advised to download the songs above, listen to them, and follow the chord progression on each to score the song. By the time you are done scoring these songs, you should have mastered the D-sharp diminished chord (D#dim) perfectly.

Note that these chord progressions are approximations; the actual chord progressions may vary depending on the specific arrangement or cover version you download. Also, note that you may need to check explanations of other chords in the songs in this course to be able to play the full chord progressions for the suggested songs.

E-Flat Diminished Chord

The E-flat diminished chord is denoted as Ebdim. You can achieve this chord by the combination of notes Eb, Gb, and Bbb. Bbb is harmonically equal to key A. This chord produces dissonance due to the stacking up of intervals at two instances, just like other minor chords.

This chord often evokes tension and instability among chord progressions. It is also useful as a safe haven to initiate modulation or transition from one key to another. It is worthy of note that despite the dissonance that this chord produces, it is also rich and useful (if deployed well and with perfect timing) for harmony and creating depth for musical arrangements. Below are pictorial representations of the E-flat diminished (Ebdim) chord.

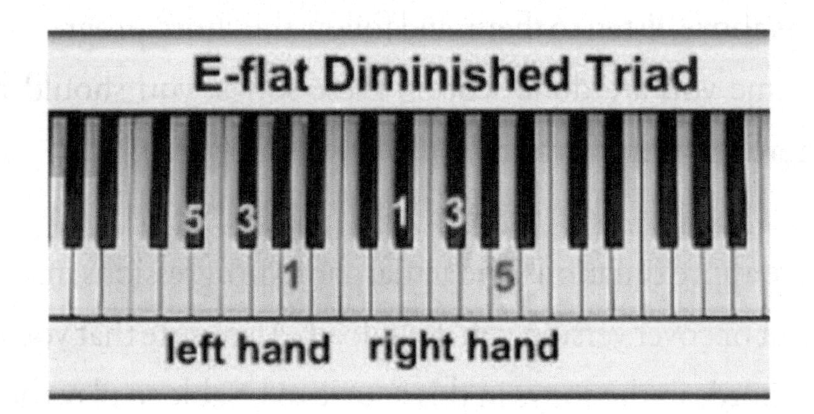

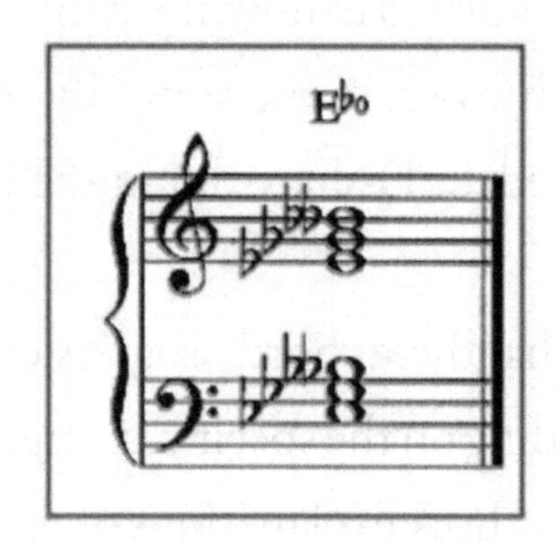

The above pictorial images are pictorial representations of E-flat diminished (Ebdim) chords on piano and music sheet.

You are advised to replicate the same on your piano and rehearse it until you get accustomed to it.

Below are examples of songs that feature E-flat diminished chords in their progressions.

1. Someone Like You" by Adele. Chord progression: Ebdim – Cm – Bb – Ab
2. "Shape of You" by Ed Sheeran. Chord progression: Ebdim – C#m – B – A
3. "Believer" by Imagine Dragon. Chord progression: Ebdim – G#m – B – F#
4. "Counting Stars" by OneRepublic. Chord progression: Ebdim – G#m – B – F#
5. "Some Nights" by Fun. Chord progression: Ebdim – Bb – Ab – Eb
6. "Jar of Hearts" by Christiana Perri. Chord progression: Ebdim – Db – Ab – Eb
7. "Rolling in the Deep" by Adele. Chord progression: Ebdim – Bb – Ab – Eb
8. "I Will Always Love You" by Whitney Houston. Chord progression: Ebdim – Db – B -Ab
9. "Lost Boy" by Ruth B. Chord progression: Ebdim - Db – Ab – Eb
10. "Fix You" Cold Play. Chord progression: Ebdim – B – Ab – F#

You are advised to download the songs above, listen to them, and follow the chord progression on each to score the song. By the time you are done scoring these songs, you should have mastered the E-flat diminished chord (Ebdim) perfectly.

Note that these chord progressions are approximations; the actual chord progressions may vary depending on the specific arrangement or cover version you download. Also, note that you may need to check explanations of other chords in the songs in this course to be able to play the full chord progressions for the suggested songs.

The E-Diminished Chord

This chord, like other diminished chords, is formed by lowering the third note by a half note and the fifth note also. An e-diminished chord that is often represented as Edim is formed in three notes, i.e., E, G, and Bb. The combination of the three notes above produces the E-diminished chord. Like its counterparts, it produces dissonance and tense quality. It is unstable, and it is moved to other stable chords when played; you can move to minor or major chords that are more stable when you play Edim, so it is mostly used as a passing chord to a stable chord or to transit to another key. Below are the pictures of Edim for you to learn and master.

E Diminished Triad

5 3 1 3

left hand right hand

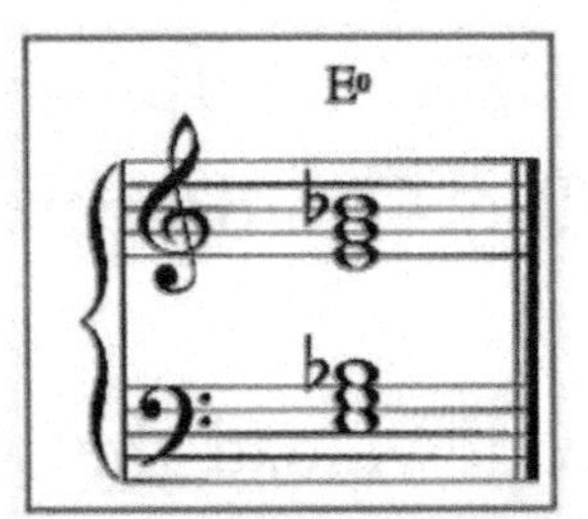

The above images are pictorial representations of the E diminished (Edim) chord on the piano and music sheet. You are advised to replicate the same on your piano and rehearse it until you get accustomed to it. Below are examples of songs that feature E-flat diminished chords in their progressions.

1. "Jerusalema" by Master KG ft. Normcebo Zikode. Cold Play. Chord progression: Edim – Bm – Em – A
2. "Ye" by Burna Boy. Chord progression: Edim – Bm – Em – A
3. "Ameno" by Era. Chord progression: Edim – B – F# - C#m
4. "Collateral Damage" by Burna Boy. Chord progression: Edim – Bm – Em – A
5. "Amaka" by 2baba ft. Peruzzi. Chord progression: Edim – Bm – Em – A

You are advised to download the songs above, listen to them, and follow the chord progression on each to score the song. By the time you are done scoring these songs, you should have mastered the E-diminished chord (Edim) perfectly. Note that these chord progressions are approximations; the actual chord progressions may vary depending on the specific arrangement or cover version you download. Also, note that you may need to check explanations of other chords in the songs in this course to be able to play the full chord progressions for the suggested songs.

F-Diminished Chord

F diminished chord is a diminished chord denoted as Fdim. It is under a triad form of chords that are realized from three notes for each chord. Fdim is realized by a combination of F, Ab, and Cb (enharmonically B). This chord functions as a passing chord and as a transitioning chord to other keys. It has a sound that can be tensed and has the potential to create harmonic complexity. Below are the pictorial representations of the F diminished chord.

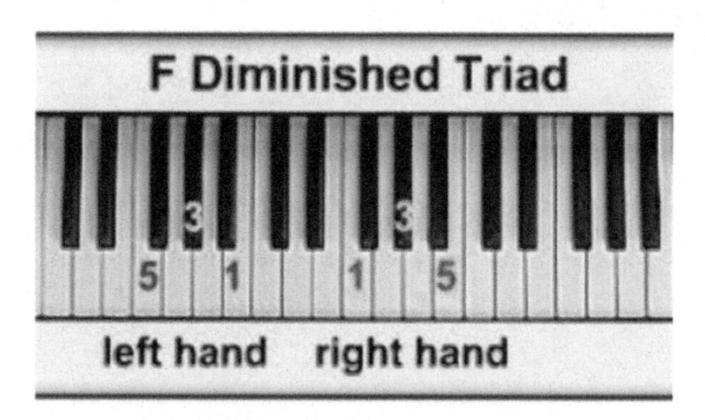

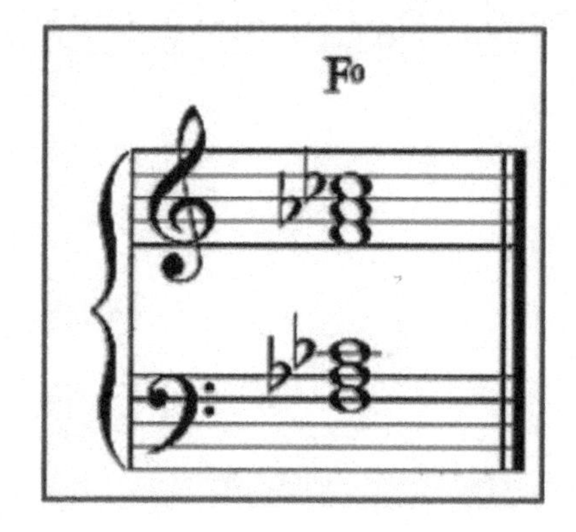

The above pictorial images are pictorial representations of F diminished (Fdim) chords on the piano and music sheet. You are advised to replicate the same on your piano and rehearse it until you get accustomed to it.

Below are examples of songs that feature F diminished chord in their progressions.

1. "Smile Like Teen Spirit" by Nirvana. Chord progression: Fdim – Bb – Ab – Db
2. "Unchained Melody" by The Righteous Brothers. Chord progression: Fdim – C – Am – Dm
3. "I Heard It Through the Grapevine" by Marvin Gaye. Chord progression: Fdim – Gm – C7 – F7
4. "Moon River" by Audrey Hepburn. Chord progression: Fdim – Dm7 – G7 – Cmaj7
5. "Don't Know Why" by Norah James. Chord progression: Fdim – Am7 – Dm7 – G7

You are advised to download the songs above, listen to them, and follow the chord progression on each to score the song. By the time you are done scoring these songs, you should have mastered the F diminished chord (Fdim) perfectly.

Note that these chord progressions are approximations; the actual chord progressions may vary depending on the specific arrangement or cover version you download. Also, note that you may need to check explanations of other chords in the songs in this course to be able to play the full chord progressions for the suggested songs.

F-Sharp Diminished Chord

The F-sharp diminished chord is a diminished chord that is formed with the combination of F#, A, and C (or enharmonically B#). F-sharp diminished chord is denoted as F#dim, constructed by putting minor intervals upon each other that results in sound dissonance and tense emotions. It can be used to substitute dominant chords. It can also be used as a passing chord to another chord, and it can be used as a transitional chord to other keys (passing chord to modulate to related keys). Below are the pictorial representations of the F-sharp diminished chord.

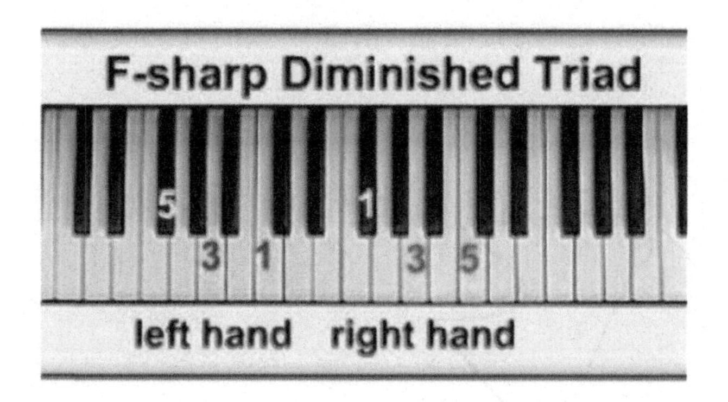

The images above are representations of F-sharp diminished (F#dim) chords on the piano and music sheet. You are advised to replicate the same on your piano and rehearse it until you get accustomed to it. Below are examples of songs that feature F-sharp diminished chords in their progressions.

Below are examples of songs that feature Fsharp diminished chords in their progressions.

1. "Suzanna" by Sauti Sol. Chord progression: F#dim – E – B – F#m
2. "Love Nwantiti" by CKay. Chord progression: F#dim – C#m – B – A
3. "Khona" by Mafikizolo ft. Uhuru. Chord progression: F#dim – E – B – F#m
4. "My Dali" by TNS ft. Indlovukazi. Chord progression: F#dim – E – B – F#m
5. "Duduke" by Simi. Chord progression: F#dim – B – E – A

You are advised to download the songs above, listen to them, and follow the chord progression on each to score the song. By the time you are done scoring these songs, you should have mastered the F-sharp diminished chord (F#dim) perfectly. Note that these chord progressions are approximations; the actual chord progressions may vary depending on the specific arrangement or cover version you download.

Also, note that you may need to check explanations of other chords in the songs in this course to be able to play the full chord progressions for the suggested songs.

G Diminished Chord

G diminished chord is symbolized as Gdim. It comprises notes G, Bb, and Db. The construction of this chord requires stacking of two minor third intervals on each other. The diminished fifth between G and Bb, as well as between the G and Db intervals, has a dissonant and tense soundIt is also used as a passing chord to other keys, creating tension in harmony before resolving to a more stable chord. Below are pictorial representations of the G diminished chord.

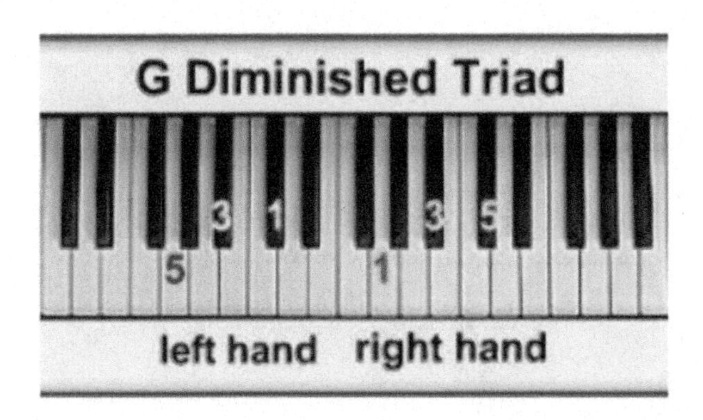

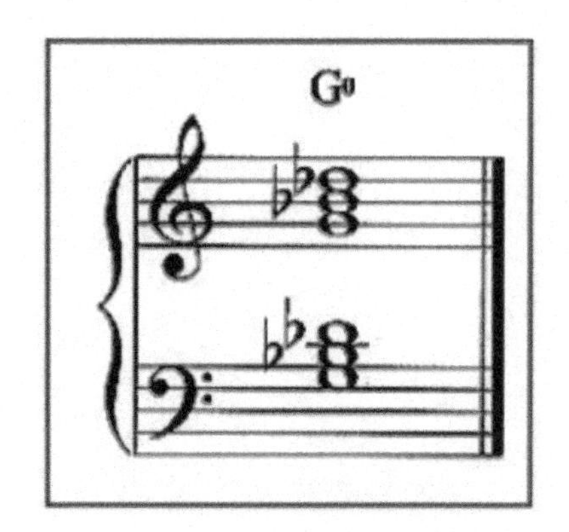

The above pictorial images are pictorial representations of G diminished (Gdim) chords on the piano and music sheet. You are advised to replicate the same on your piano and rehearse it for some time till you get accustomed to it.

Below are examples of songs that feature G diminished chord in their progressions.

1. "Big Bang" by Bullet Train. Chord progression: G – Gdim – Am – D
2. "DNA" by BTS. Chord progression: G – Gdim – Em – C
3. "Tennis Court" by Lorde. Chord progression: G – Gdim – Em – C
4. "Tala" by Sarah Geronimo. Chord progression: G – Gdim – Em – C
5. "Tadow" by Masego & FKJ. Chord progression: G – Gdim – Am – D

You are advised to download the songs above, listen to them, and follow the chord progression on each to score the song. By the time you are done scoring these songs, you should have mastered the G diminished chord (Gdim) perfectly.

Note that these chord progressions are approximations; the actual chord progressions may vary depending on the specific arrangement or cover version you download. Also, note that you may need to check explanations of other chords in the songs in this course to be able to play the full chord progressions for the suggested songs.

G Sharp Diminished Chord

G-sharp diminished chord, often denoted as G#dim by piano players consists of notes G#, B, and D. Like other diminished chords, minor thirds intervals are stacked together on top of each other. The diminished fifth between G# and B, as well as between G# and D interval, has an effect, and the effect is dissonance and tense sound. It is also used as a passing chord to other keys, creating tension in harmony before resolving to a more stable chord. Below are pictorial representations of the G-sharp diminished (G#dim) chord.

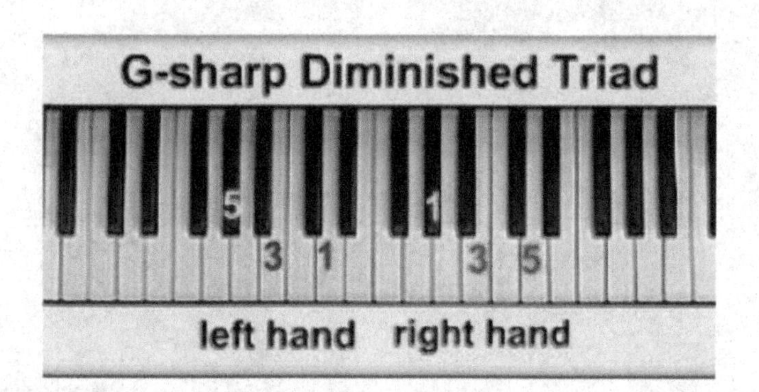

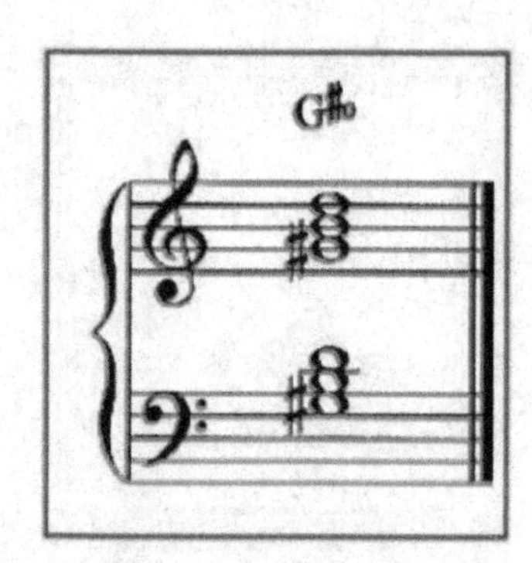

The above images are pictorial representations of G-sharp diminished (G#dim) chords on the piano and music sheet. You are advised to replicate the same on your piano and rehearse it until you get accustomed to it. Below are examples of songs that feature G-sharp diminished chords in their progressions.

Below are examples of songs that feature Gsharp diminished chords in their progressions.

1. "Volare" by Dean Martins. Chord progression: G – G#dim – Am – D7 – G
2. "Corazon Espinado" by Santana ft. Mana. Chord progression: Em – G#dim – Am – B7 –Em
3. "Libertango" by Astor Piazolla (Tango). Chord progression: Dm – G#dim – Am – G#dim– Dm
4. "Corcovado" by Antonio Carlos Jobim. Chord progression: Am7 – G#dim7 – Am7 – G#dim7 – Am7
5. "Europa" by Santa. Chord progression: Em – G#dim – Am – G#dim – Em

You are advised to download the songs above, listen to them, and follow the chord progression on each to score the song. By the time you are done scoring these songs, you should have mastered the G-sharp diminished chord (G#dim) perfectly. Note that these chord progressions are approximations; the actual chord progressions may vary depending on the specific arrangement or cover version you download.

Also, note that you may need to check explanations of other chords in the songs in this course to be able to play the full chord progressions for the suggested songs.

A Diminished Chord

The A diminished chord is a diminished chord that is formed with notes A, C, and Eb. It can be used to add drama and suspense to musical compositions due to its character of tension and unstableness. Below are the pictorial representations of A diminished chord.

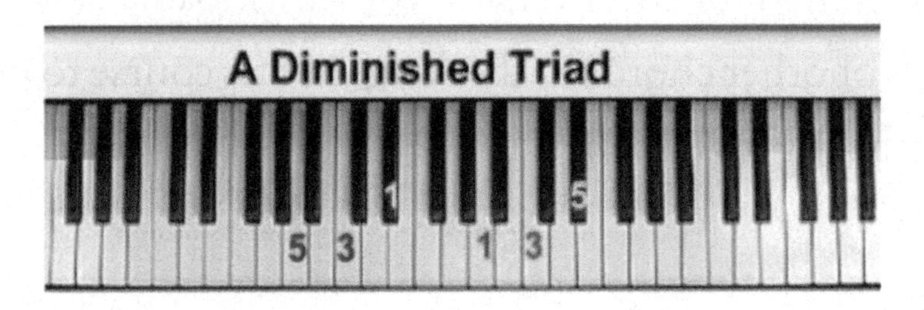

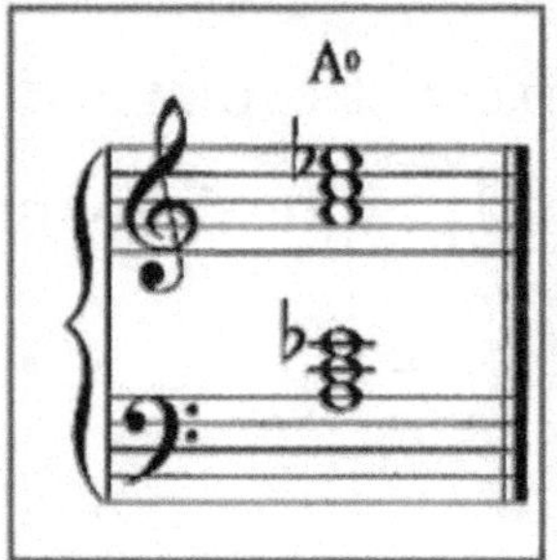

The above images are pictorial representations of an A diminished (A-dim) chord on the piano and a music sheet. You are advised to replicate the same on your piano and rehearse it until you get accustomed to it. Below are examples of songs that feature A diminished chord in their progressions.

Below are examples of songs that feature A diminished chord in their progressions.

1. "So What" by Miles Davis. Chord progression: Dm7 – Adim7 – Dm7 – Adim7 – Em7 – Adim7 – Em7 – Adim7
2. "Afor Blue" by Mongo Santamaria. Chord progression: Dm7 – Adim7 – Dm7 – Adim7 – Em7 – Adim7 – Em7 – Adim7
3. "St. Thomas" by Sonny Rollins. Chord progression: C – G7 – C – Adim7 – Dm7 – G7 – C
4. "Manteca" by Dizzy Gillespie. Chord progression: Bbm7 – Bdim7 – Am7 – D7 – Gm7 – C7
5. "All of Me" by John Legend. Chord progression: Am – Adim – G – Em – F – C – Dm – E7

You are advised to download the songs above, listen to them, and follow the chord progression on each to score the song. By the time you are done scoring these songs, you should have mastered A diminished chord (Adim) perfectly.

Note that these chord progressions are approximations; the actual chord progressions may vary depending on the specific arrangement or cover version you download. Also, note that you may need to check explanations of other chords in the songs in this course to be able to play the full chord progressions for the suggested songs.

A-Sharp Diminished Chord

The A-sharp diminished chord, like the other diminished chords, is formed by stacking minor third intervals on top of each other. It creates dissonance accompanied by tense quality as a result of a diminished fifth interval. The notes that forms the A-sharp diminished (A#dim) chord are A#, C#, and E. Below are the pictorial representations of the A-sharp diminished chord.

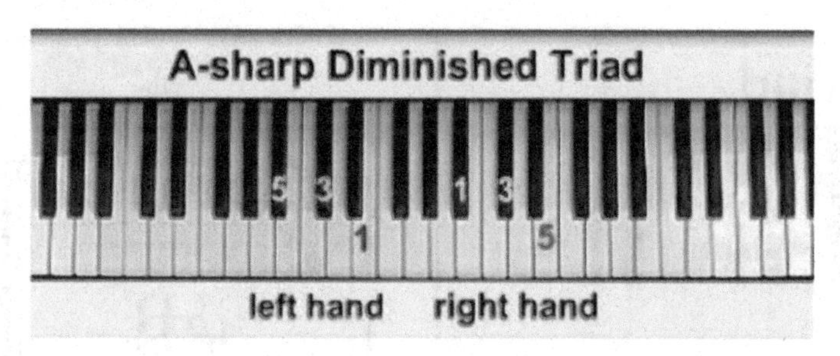

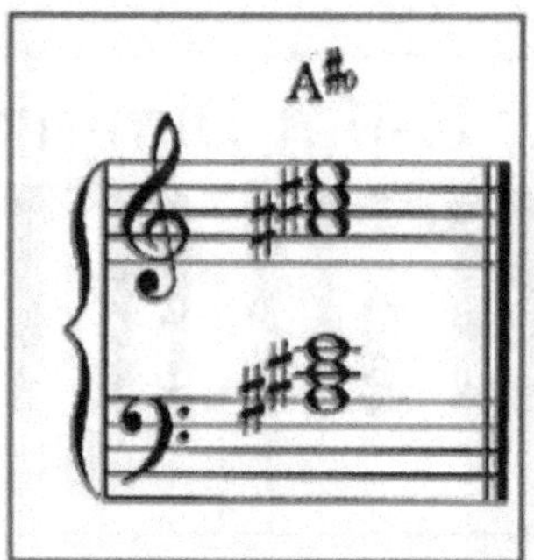

The above images are pictorial representations of A-sharp diminished (A#dim) chords on the piano and music sheet. You are advised to replicate the same on your piano and rehearse it for some time till you get it and get accustomed to it.

Below are examples of songs that feature A# diminished chord (A#dim) in their progressions.

1. "La Isla Bonita" by Madonna. Chord progression: C – A#dim – F – G – C
2. "Smooth Operator" by Sade. Chord progression: Dm – A#dim – Dm – A#dim – Dm
3. "Tuyo" by Rodrigo Amarante. Chord progression: Dm – A#dim – Gm – C7 – F
4. "Adios Nonino" by Astor Piazzola. Chord progression: Dm – A#dim – Dm – A#dim – Dm
5. "Besame Muncho" by Consuelo Velazquez. Chord progression: Am – A#dim – Bm – E7 – Am

You are advised to download the songs above, listen to them, and follow the chord progression on each to score the song. By the time you are done scoring these songs, you should have mastered the A-sharp diminished chord (A#dim) perfectly. Note that these chord progressions are approximations; the actual chord progressions may vary depending on the specific arrangement or cover version you download. Also, note that you may need to check explanations of other chords in the songs in this course to be able to play the full chord progressions for the suggested songs.

B-Flat Diminished Chord

The B-flat diminished chord is symbolized as Bbdim. It is formed from three notes of B-flat, D-flat, and F. This chord, like other diminished chords, generates a tense atmosphere and dissonance. It is used across various genres and music styles. Below are the pictorial representations of the B-flat diminished chord.

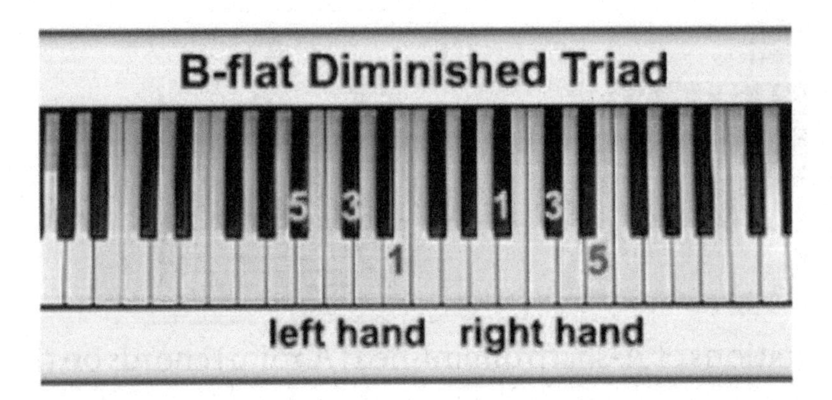

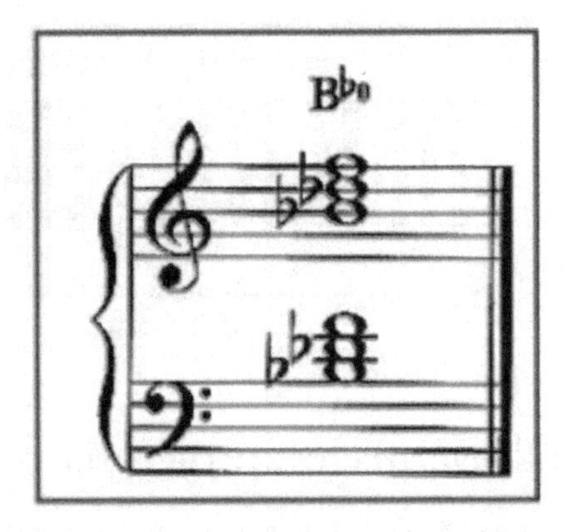

The above images are pictorial representations of B-flat diminished (Bbdim) chords on piano and music sheets. You are advised to replicate the same on your piano and rehearse it for some time till you master and get accustomed to it.

Below are examples of songs that feature the Bb diminished chord (Bbdim) in their progressions.

1. "Someone Like You" by Adele. Chord progression: G – Bbdim – Am – C – G/B – B – C – D
2. "La Vie en Rose" by Edith Piaf. Chord progression: C – Bbdim – Am – D7 – G – G7 – C
3. What a Wonderful World" by Louis Armstrong. Chord progression: F – Fmaj7 – Bbdim –C7 – F – Fmaj7 – Bbdim – C7
4. "Georgia on My Mind" by Ray Charles. Chord progression: C – E7 – A7 – D7 – Gm7 – C7 – F – F#dim7 – C
5. "Take Five" by Dave Brubeck. Chord progression: Ebm – Dbsus4 – Bbdim7 – Ab7 – Gb

You are advised to download the songs above, listen to them, and follow the chord progression on each to score the song. By the time you are done scoring these songs, you should have mastered the B-flat diminished chord (Bbdim) perfectly.

Note that these chord progressions are approximations; the actual chord progressions may vary depending on the specific arrangement or cover version you download. Also, note that you may need to check explanations of other chords in the songs in this course to be able to play the full chord progressions for the suggested songs.

B-Diminished Chord

A B diminished chord is often denoted as Bdim. It is a triad chord that is characterized by suspense, tension, and instability in a piece or musical composition. It is formed from three notes of B, D, and F. Looking at the formation, you will see that it is formed by stacking up minor third intervals on top of each other. It also can be introduced into a composition to add a form of complexity and depth to the composition. Below are the pictorial representations of the chord.

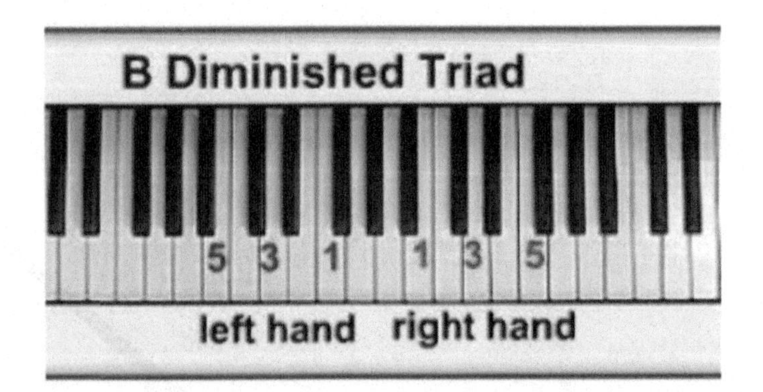

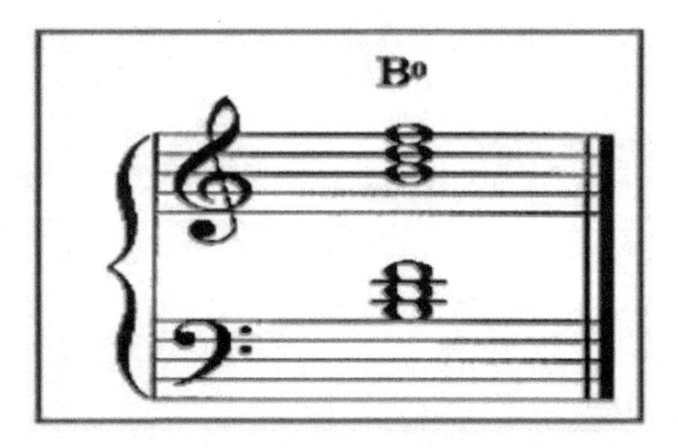

The above images are pictorial representations of a B diminished (Bdim) chord on the piano and music sheet. You are advised to replicate the same on your piano and rehearse it until you get accustomed to it.

Below are examples of songs that feature Bb diminished chord (Bdim) in their progressions.

1. "Sakura" by Ketsumeishi. Chord progression: B – Bdim – E – F# - B – F# - B – F# - E –Bdim
2. "Ti Amo" by Exo. Chord progression: Am – C – G – Bdim – Em – Am
3. "Kiss Me" by Sixpence None the Richer. Chord progression: G – D – Em – Bdim – C – G – C – G
4. "Bad Liar" by Imagine Dragon. Chord progression: D – A – Bm – G – D – A – Bm – G – Bdim
5. "Turning Back to You" by Mayday. Chord progression: G – D – Em – Bdim – C – G – D

You are advised to download the songs above, listen to them, and follow the chord progression on each to score the song. By the time you are done scoring these songs, you should have mastered the B diminished chord (Bdim) perfectly. Note that these chord progressions are approximations; the actual chord progressions may vary depending on the specific arrangement or cover version you download.

Also, note that you may need to check explanations of other chords in the songs in this course to be able to play the full chord progressions for the suggested songs.

Note: From this level onward, you are advised to search online for examples where the chords were discussed, and its features; then apply them in learning on your piano. Now, you're able to search for examples on your own and follow the former principles learned to play songs. Below we will be discussing more about chords.

AUGMENTED CHORD

Augmented chords produce a sound of tension and instability in music. This effect makes them important as they are deployed to evoke emotions and feelings of tension and instability before a more stable chord that evokes feelings of ease, calmness, stability, and joy; for instance, a major chord can be played immediately after them. Since you've learned about diminished chords, it shouldn't be difficult to grasp augmented chords.

To understand an augmented chord, see it as the "bigger" or "wider" counterpart of the diminished chord. Augmented chords follow almost the same pattern as diminished chords, with slightly a difference between the two. In an augmented triad, we take a major chord and then raise the fifth by half-step. So, we have root notes, major third, and augmented fifth. We have 12 augmented triads on piano, and these are C, C#, D, D#, E, F, F#, G, G#, A, and B. Relax and check out the explanations below on to how to play all of the augmented chords. Note that the keys painted in red are the keys you will combine to form the chords to be discussed.

C Augmented Chord (C Aug or C+)

The C augmented chord is also widely represented as either C Aug or C+ among music professionals. The C-augmented chord consists of three notes. These notes are C, E, and G#. This chord is used to create dissonance and tension. It is also useful for chromatic movement in a bit to add color, depth, and unstable sound to music before a chord for resolution is played. Check the C Aug's picture below and copy the same on your piano.

C Aug Chord Picture

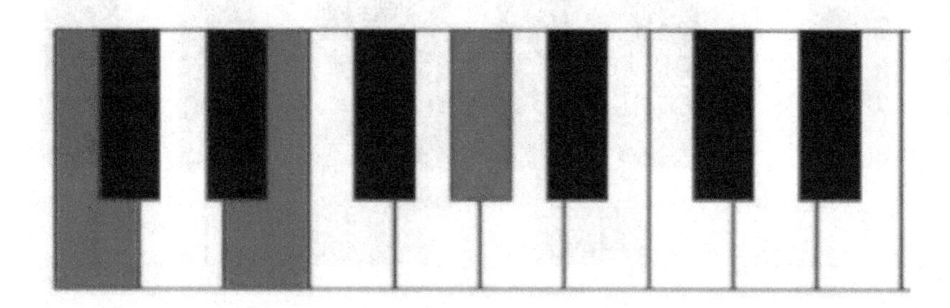

D Augmented Chord

The D augmented chord is often symbolized by either D+ or Daug. It comprises the combination of D, F#, and A#. Like other augmented chords, it produces tension and instability in music. It is frequently used for chromatic transition or modulation to other keys in a bit to deliver bold and unsettled tones in musical compositions and progressions. Below is the picture of Daug on piano.

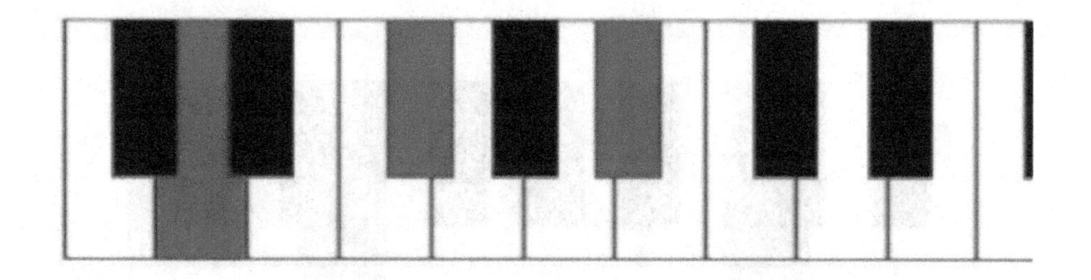

D Sharp Augmented Chord

D-sharp augmented chord is denoted as D+ or Daug in music. As the triad that it is, three notes are combined to form this chord, and they are D# (the root note), G (the major third), and B (the diminished fifth). It can be used for chromatic progression to add flair and complexity to a musical composition. Below is the pictorial representation of the D-sharp diminished chord.

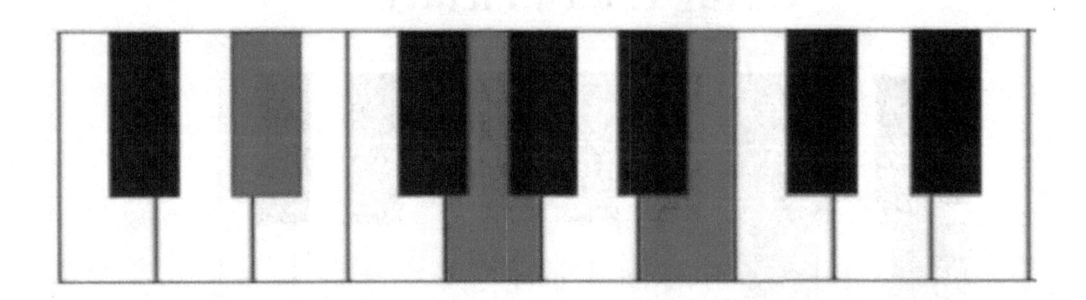

E Augmented Chord

The E augmented chord is also denoted as E Aug or E+ by musicians and instrumentalists. Like other triads, it is formed with the combination of three notes of E (as the root note), G# (the perfect fifth), and C (the diminished fifth). It is also often used for chromatic progression and to introduce a tense mood before a resolving chord is used. Below is the diagram of this chord. Kindly model on it to master it on your piano.

F Augmented Chord

The F augmented chord is usually denoted as F Aug or F+. It is a triad that consists of notes F (the root note), A (the major third), and C# (the diminished fifth). It can be used to add color, brightness, vibrancy, and tension to a musical composition. It is also used as chromatic movement and to transit to other related keys. Below is a pictorial example of how to play this chord.

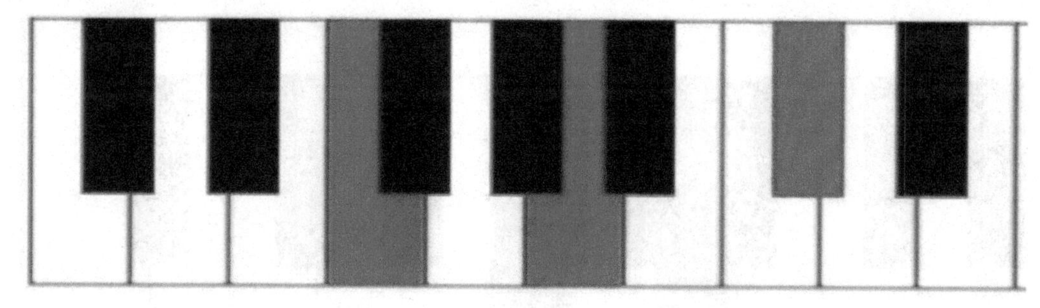

F# Augmented Chord

The F-sharp augmented chord is also denoted as either F# Aug or F#+. It is formed from the combination of three notes as a triad. The notes/keys are F# as the root note, A# as its major third, and D as its diminished fifth. Like other diminished chords, it does the same work of adding color, tension, and instability to musical compositions. Check the diagram below to replicate the same on your piano.

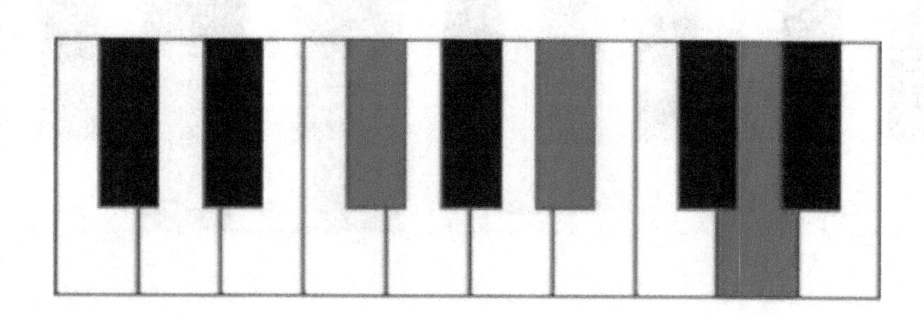

G Augmented Chord

The G augmented chord is a triad, likewise, with the combination of notes G, B, and D#. The interval between the root chord G and the diminished fifth D# produces a tense sound and dissonance. This sound is useful for chromatic playing, modulation, and creating tension before a resolution in a musical composition. Below is the pictorial representation of the diagram to be replicated by you on your piano. Follow the painted red keys.

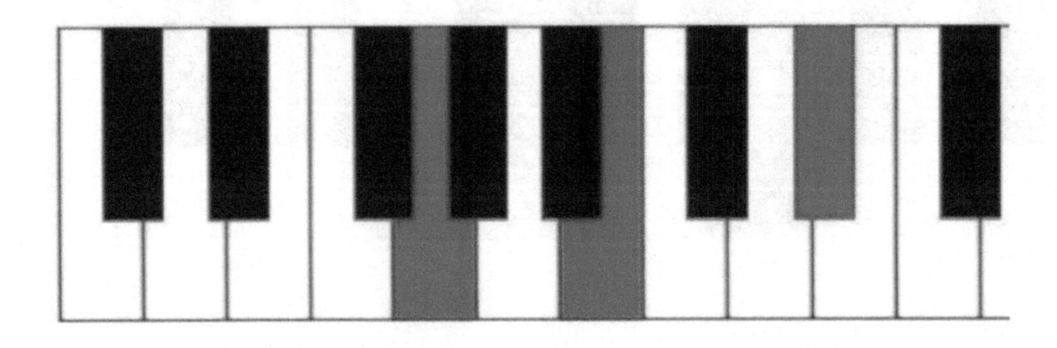

G-Sharp Augmented Chord

The G-sharp augmented chord is widely recognized as either G# Aug or G#+. It comprises G#, B#, and E to create the G# Aug chord noted for its dissonance, chromatic movement, and adding of color and depth to musical compositions. Below is a picture of it on the keyboard for you to replicate. The correct combinations are marked with red.

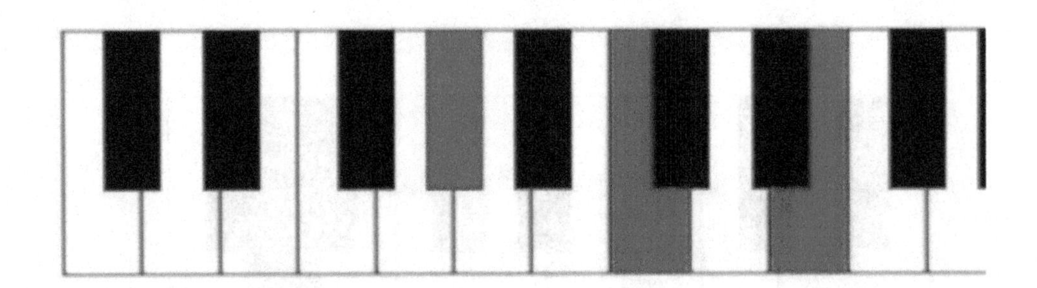

The A Augmented Chord

The A augmented chord is denoted as A aug or A+. It contains A, C#, and E# as a triad. Like other augmented chords discussed earlier, it is noted for its dissonance, chromatic movement, and adding of color and depth to musical compositions. Below is a picture of it on the keyboard for you to replicate. The correct combinations are marked with red.

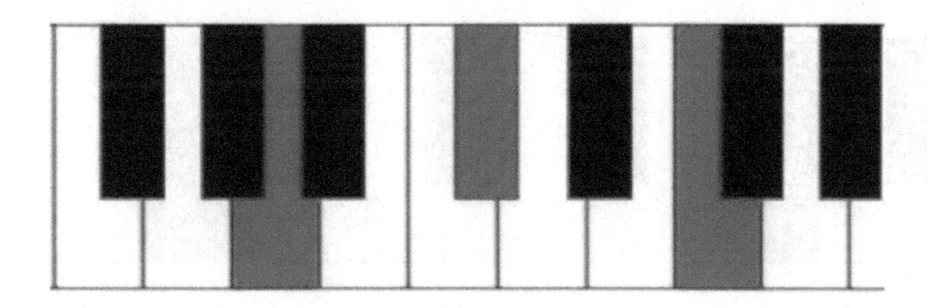

A-Sharp Augmented Chord

The A-sharp diminished chord is denoted and uses symbols of either A# Aug or A#+. It comprises three notes played together to realize it, and these notes are A#, D, and F#. It is noted for its dissonance, chromatic movement, adding of color and depth to musical compositions. Below is a picture of it on the keyboard for you to replicate. The correct combinations are marked with red.

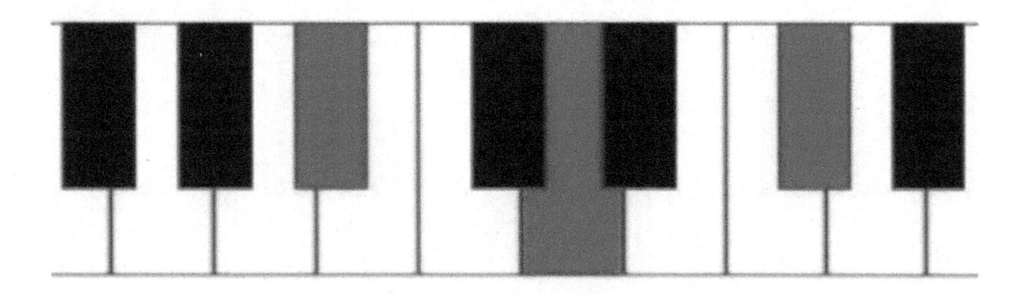

B Augmented Chord

The B augmented chord is also denoted as B Aug or B+. It consists of notes B, D#, and G. The notes above are the root, the major third, and the diminished fifth, respectively. It is noted for its dissonance, chromatic movement and adding of color and depth to musical compositions. Below is a picture of it on the keyboard for you to replicate. The correct combinations are marked with red

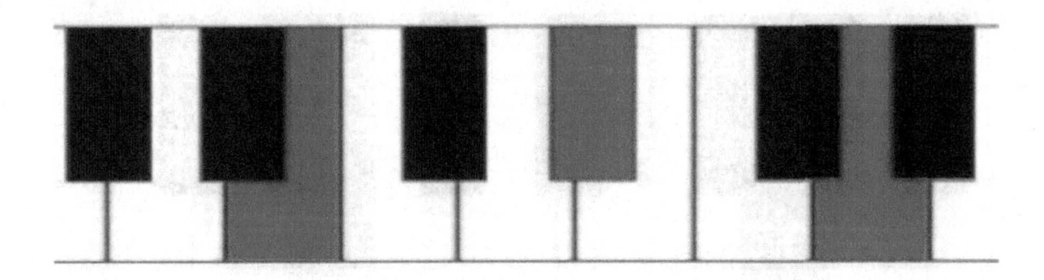

THE 7TH CHORD AND CHORD EXTENSIONS

01 When we say 7th chord in piano playing, what do we mean? A 7th chord is a chord of four notes that has a root, a major or minor third, a perfect fifth, and a minor seventh just above the root. They are used extensively in Jazz, blues, pop, etc. Its richness and complexity are the outcomes of the seventh interval. Common types of the 7th chords are dominant 7th (major triad with minor seventh), major 7th (major triad with major seventh), and minor triad (minor triad with minor seventh).

We have six variants of the 7th chord. For this level, we will be treating the three most common variants, which are the Dominant 7th chord (7), Major seventh chords (maj7), and Minor seventh chord (m7). Check the formula for each variant and master them. You will be given some examples so that you can complete the rest during your practice time.

The major 7th Chord (Maj7) formula is 1:3:5:7. Examples of this are Cmaj7 with notes C, E, G, and B. Check the diagram below and follow suit. The diagram below is the **Cmaj7 chord.**

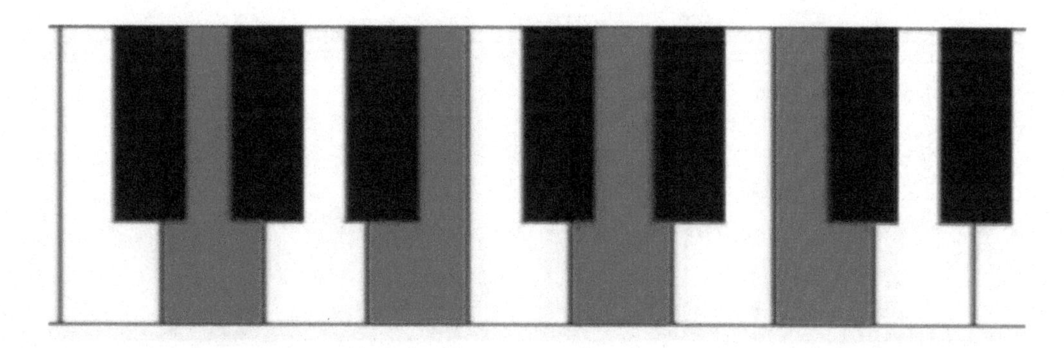

02 The dominant 7th chord (7) formula is 1:3:5:b7. An example of the dominant 7th chord is the G7 with notes G – B – D – F. The diagram below displays **the G7 dominant chord.**

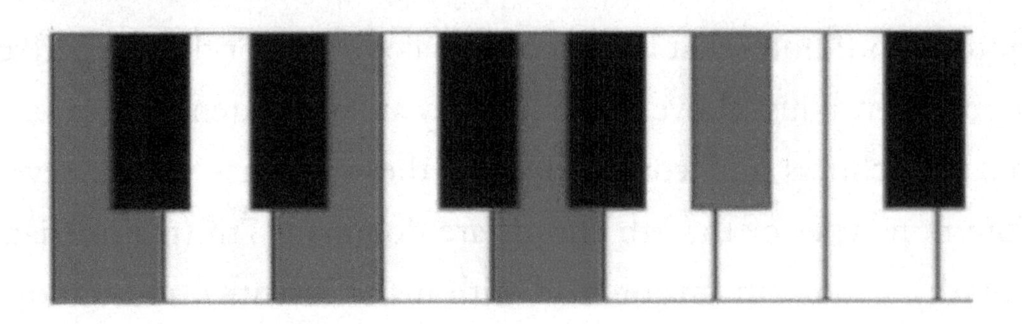

03 The minor 7th chord (m7) formula is 1 – b3 – 5 – b7. An example of a minor 7th chord (m7) is Dm7 with notes Dm – F – A – C. Check the formula and see how you can locate others, likewise. Below is **Dm7** on a piano as a pictorial example.

These are the most common three. After these three, comes half diminished 7th chord and fully diminished 7th chord. The formula and examples of both are given below.

1. Half diminished 7th chord (m7b5) formula is 1 – b3 – b5 – b7. An example of this is the **F#m7b5 (F-sharp minor7 flat-5).** Check below for the pictorial representation of this for better comprehension.

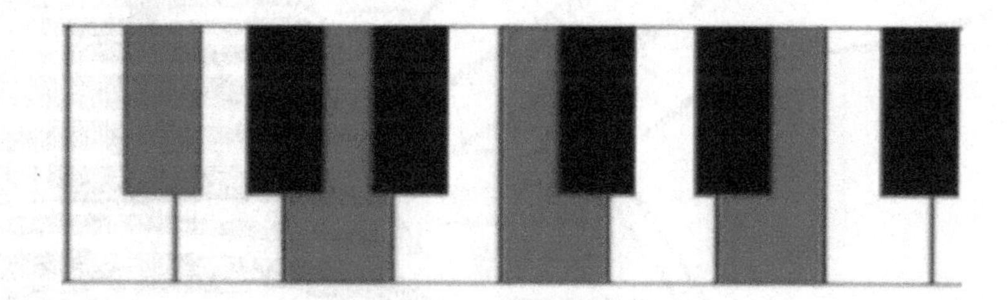

2. A Fully diminished 7th chord (dim7) formula is 1 – b3 – b5 – bb7 (or 6). Applying this formula for the A7dim chord will give you these notes: A – C – Eb – Gb. Below is the pictorial example of an A7dim chord on the piano. You are advised to follow this diagram of the A7dim chord and the formula above to learn the rest

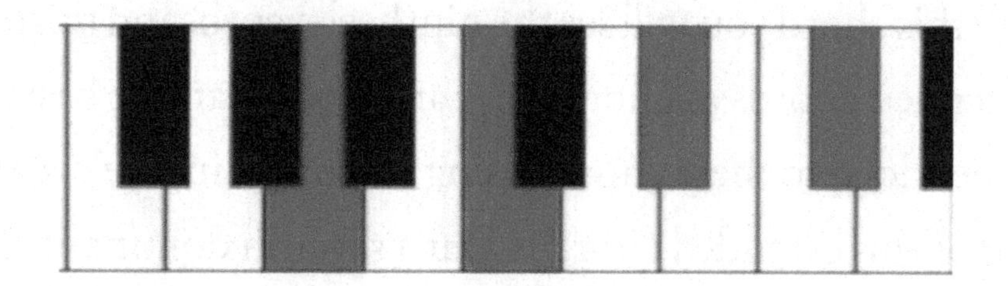

CHORD EXTENSION

As the name implies, chord extension are extended chords with one or more thirds one octave higher. It is with this chord you will see the ninth, eleventh, and thirteenth chords. To make it simple, see extended chords as chords that are more than the basic triads (3 notes). Additional notes can be added to these chords using seventh, ninth, eleventh, or thirteenth intervals. The concept of this extended chord is that a seventh dominant chord is extended with a major third to create a ninth chord. A ninth chord could also be extended with a minor third to build an eleventh chord.

Finally, you can extend an eleventh chord to build a thirteenth chord by adding a major third. We have covered the seventh chords in our previous unit; we will now focus on the ninth, eleventh, and thirteen chords. Check the examples of extended chords with pictures below to have a good grasp of the theory above.

The Ninth Chords

The ninth chords are the chords that contain the root note, third, fifth, and ninth interval. Common ninth chords include major9 (major triad with major 7th and major 9th), dominant 9th (major triad with minor 7th and major 9th), and minor 9th (minor triad with minor 7th and major 9th). Below are some examples of ninth chords in pictures.

C9 Chord or Dominant 9th Chord (Example of a Ninth Chord

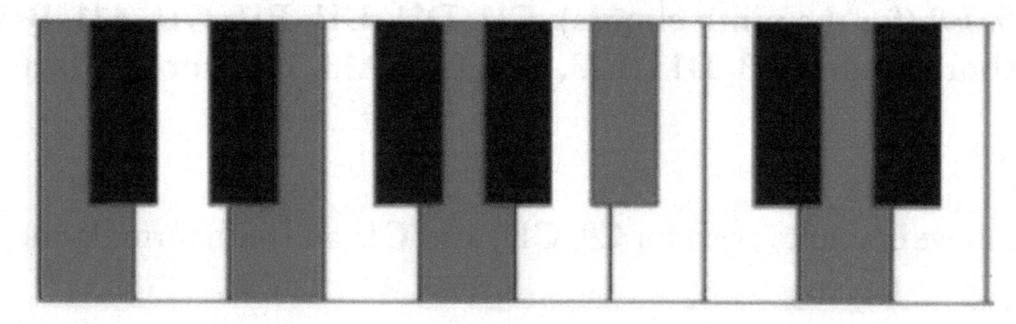

The notes for the C9 chord above are C, E, G, Bb, and D

C11 chord (example of an eleventh chord)

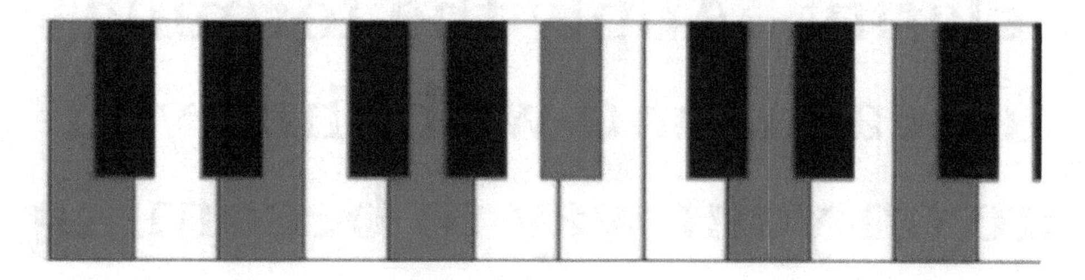

The notes for the C11 chord above are C, E, G, Bb, D, and F.

C13 chord (example of a 13th chord)

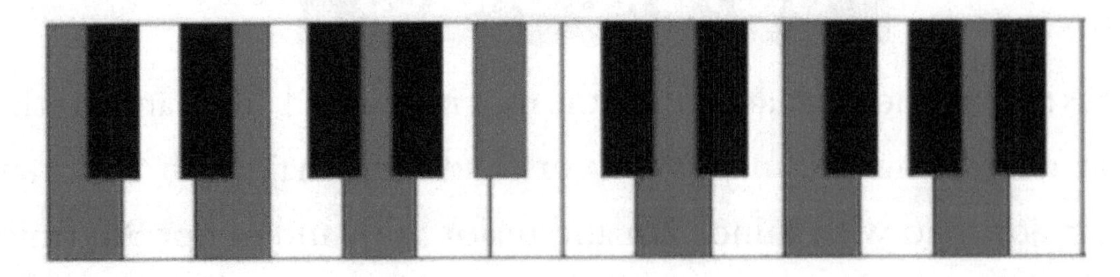

The notes for the C13 chord above are C, E, G, Bb, D, F, and A.

The ninth, eleventh, and thirteenth chords we have as per piano playing are **C9, D9, E9, F9, G9, A9, B9 (for the ninth chords), C11, D11, E11, F11, G11, A11, B11 (for the eleventh chords), and C13, D13, E13, F13, G13, A13, B13 (for the thirteenth chords).**

Follow the above examples given for **C9, C11, and C13** and with formula and explanation to get others.

Read the theory again in case of any confusion or for clarity. Apply the formula for each, and with this, you are on your way to becoming a real intermediary piano player with a piano-player mode activated.

OTHER TYPES OF CHORD

We've been discussing the most important chords for an intermediate player, but you will be a better piano player if you know the other chords at this stage because they are supposed to be taught to early, advanced or professional piano players. We will briefly discuss the chords, which call "other chords," in this course.

The other chords are Diatonic chords, Slash chords, "Sus" chords, and "Add" chords. Let's take them one after the other.

Diatonic Chords: When we say diatonic chords, we talk about chords that belong only to a certain key and are built using only notes you can find on the same key's scale. In other words, diatonic chords are chords that naturally occur on a certain scale, and these chords align with the scale's key signature. These chords follow the pattern of **three major chords (I, IV, V), three minor chords (ii, iii, VI), and one diminished chord.** The pattern that follows can also be written **as major-minor-minor-major-major-minor-diminished.** By following the above formula and guidelines, the diatonic chord in the key of C major would be **Cmaj (I), Dmin (ii), Emin (iii), Fmaj (IV), Gmaj (V), Amin (iv), and Bdim.** Pictorial examples of diatonic chords are given below. You are advised to follow the explanation and formula above to get the rest on your own.

Pictorial example of C diatonic chords

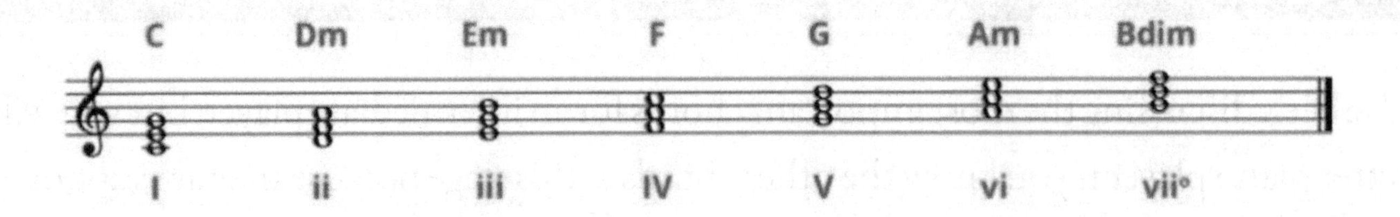

Pictorial example of F diatonic chords

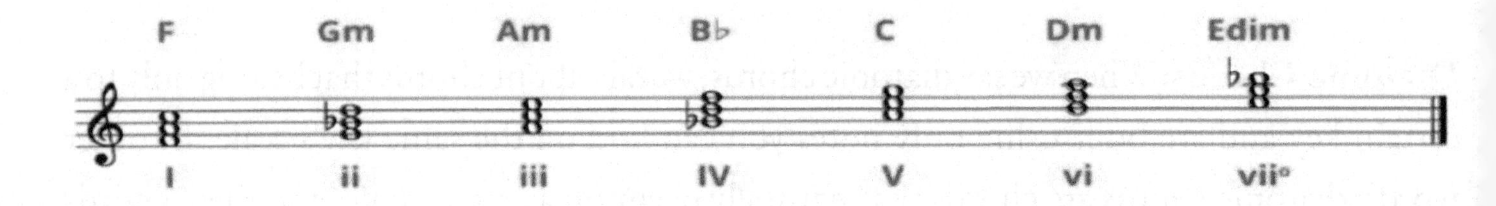

SLASH CHORDS

This type of chord is technical. A slash chord resembles a combination of chord symbols and a single note. In the "slash" chord, you will see a slash (/) between chord symbols.

When you see this, it gives you further information about what you should play with your right and left hands.

Simply put, a slash chord is a chord where a different note than the root is played at the lowest pitch, and a slash is usually used to divide the chord symbols to be played by both hands. For instance, if you see a slash chord written as C/E, you are being instructed to play a C chord with your right hand and note E as a bass note on your left hand. Check out the picture below for better comprehension.

Pictorial example of Slash C/E chord

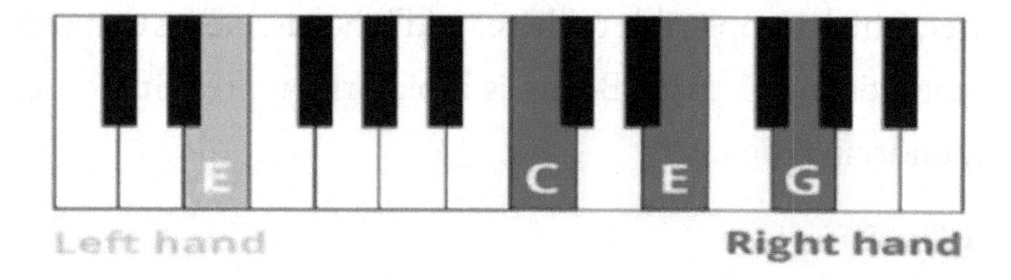

"SUS" CHORDS

The "Sus" chord is a shortened form of what is known as "suspended chords" in piano playing. When we substitute one tone for another in the middle of a song, we create a suspended melody. We have what is known as sus2 and sus4. You have sus2 when you replace the third note with the second note close to the root. And in a sus4, you replace the third with the fourth note from the root. Check the example below to get a grasp of what sus2 and sus4 denote, respectively.

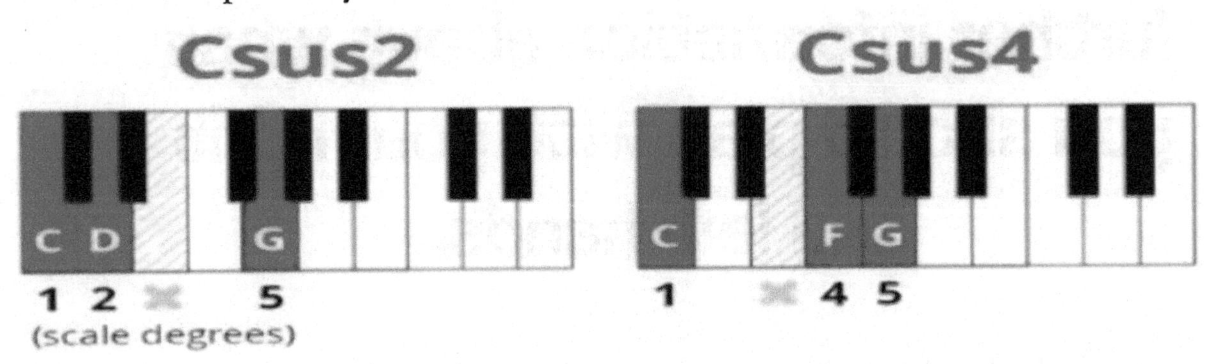

"ADDS" CHORDS

Like the chord discussed above, the word "adds" is a shortened form of the word "additional." It means that you are expected to add an extra tone on top of your existing triad without altering the chord's fundamental quality. It would help if you were careful to distinguish this chord in symbols from other chords that may look familiar. For instance, you can see Cmaj9 and Cadd9. You should know that the former includes whole stacks of thirds, while the latter, which is applicable to these "add" chords, means that you should add the ninth tone to the existing C triad. Below is a pictorial representation of the above explanation for easy understanding.

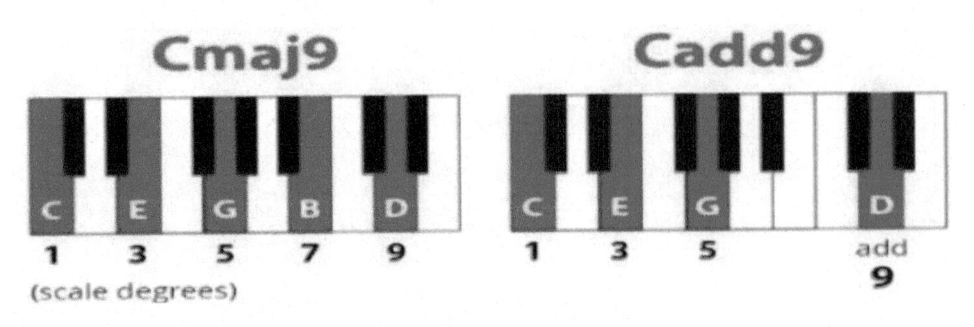

PEDALING AND PEDALING TECHNIQUES

What is Pedaling in Piano?

To answer this question, we must know what a pedal is in a piano. A pedal is a foot controller that alters the piano's sound so that a player can easily add tone, character, and artistic expressions to piano playing and sound effortlessly. So, pedaling in piano refers to the common technique of using a sustain or damper pedal in a bid to sustain or dampen the sound of the notes being played. Notably, most "personal" keyboards and pianos do not usually come with pedals.

The idea of a pedal is more common with pianists and organists than with others. Though you can go ahead and purchase your pedals and fix them with your keyboard to play, the ones that are played with grand pianos are arguably the best form of pedal.

We have three types of pedals in piano playing:

- Soft pedal or una corda: these pedals are arranged from left to right.
- The sostenuto pedal and
- The damper pedal (or damper pad)

One of which might be that the player does not see any need for it or some time to create an effect such as muting function, also known as "silent piano." B Below is a pictorial representation of the arrangement of pedals.

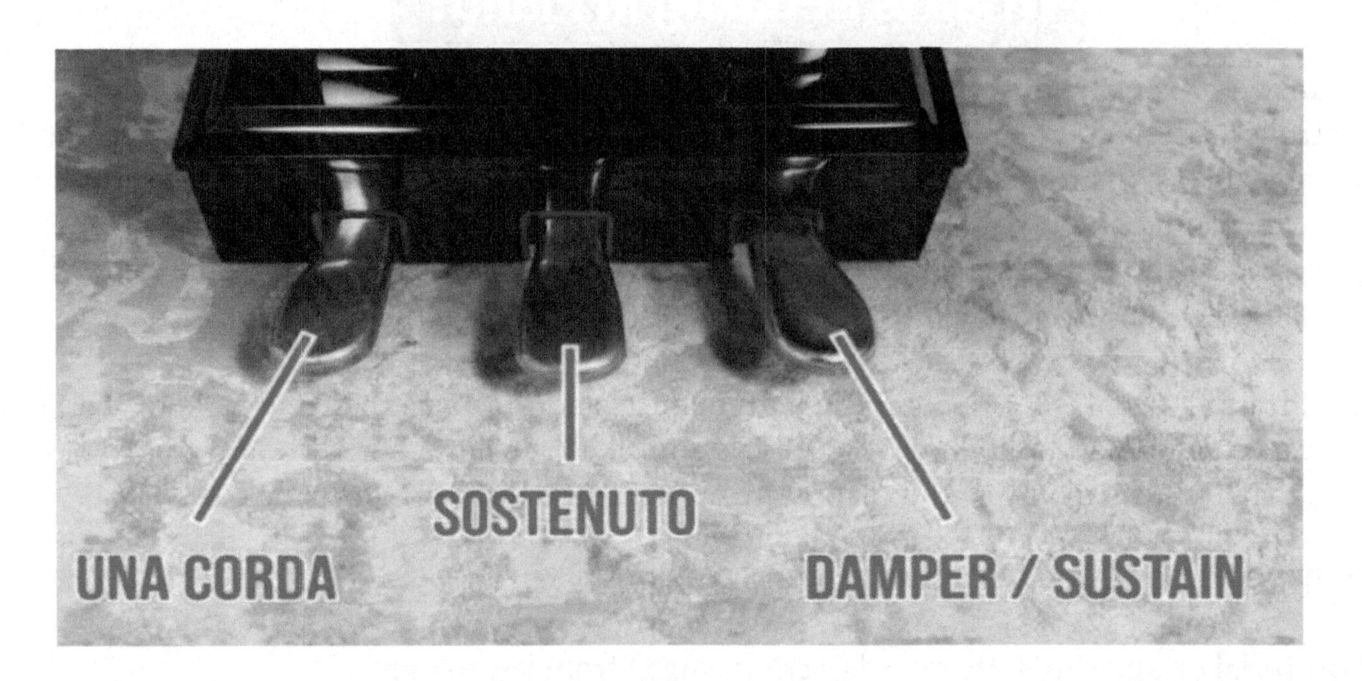

Mastering the correct pedaling technique is very crucial for any pianist who wants to improve and hone their skills as a professional piano player because the three pedals (sustain or damper, una corda, and sostenuto) play a vital role in shaping how the piano will sound, its dynamics, and overall emotions.

Since each pedal is distinct and has certain functions and effects, we must master the correct techniques applicable to each of them so that you can be able to apply them correctly to get your desired results from using them.

Let's talk about the most common of the three first. It is called a damper or sustain pedal. It is the most common, and it is usually pressed with the right foot. It has the primary function of sustaining the sounds of notes. You should press this pedal smoothly and release clearly to make sure the music isn't muddy or creating excessive resonance, it should be clear to the ears instead.

Also, we have the soft pedal (Unal Corda Pedal) on the other hand. This is to be operated by your left foot.

Note that the word una corda means "one string." It creates soft sounds by shifting the entire keyboard to the right so that the hammers will strike fewer strings per note. This should be pressed only when you need such effects or outcomes that we stated earlier above. You should press it gently and softly to avoid muddling the sounds up or reducing the quality of tone and or dynamic controls.

Lastly, the sostenuto is a pedal that is less used by pianists compared to the two discussed earlier. It is usually found on grand pianos. This pedal is only used when you want to give the effect of sustenance to the only notes you hold down. The few notes you hold will be sustained when you use this pedal. In contrast, the notes you play immediately after will decay.

Examples of Pedaling

The examples of pedaling to be discussed in this session are half-pedaling syncopated pedaling, and staccato pedaling. Let's take them one after the other and explain each.

Half Pedaling

This half pedalling technique is used when a pianist wants to sustain specific notes from other notes played at the same time. You use half pedaling to sustain the notes you want so that other notes played that are unwanted would fade off (decay). In other words, half-pedaling will mean that the pianist depresses the sustained pedal halfway or to a degree to allow control over sustained notes. This technique's desired effect is to sustain sounds that the pianist holds to varying degrees.

Syncopated Pedaling

Syncopated pedaling is a technique of pedaling that we use to coordinate the movement of the damper or sustain pedal to achieve rhythm patterns and artistic expression of the music we play. For instance, where the pedal changes occur on strong beats or at the start of measures, syncopated pedaling is the introduction of pedal changes on off beats or in between beats sometimes; it creates syncopation. The function of syncopated pedaling is to dim that may exist between changes in harmony and accents of rhythm to add a sense of fluidity and motions to music. Musical rhythmic vitality, energy, sense of momentum, and performance may be enhanced in people when the pedal is rightly and strategically synced.

Staccato Pedaling

Staccato pedaling is a technique that creates an effect known as "staccato." Staccato pedaling is when you press the sustain pedal (damper) quickly and detachably to create a short, crisp, and percussion sound while maintaining a degree of resonance and smooth/blending between notes. Using this technique would help if you are always careful not to muddle notes or chords

For instance, by lifting the pedal immediately and quickly depressing it for the next sets of notes, you can achieve a very clean, articulated sound with just a very subtle sense of sustain.

DIVERSIFYING REPERTOIRE

What are the Different Musical Genres for an Intermediate to Explore?

At the start of this course, we provided in great detail explanations on who an intermediate player is. One of the distinct characteristics of an intermediate piano player is that such a person is well versed in different genres and styles of music. The various genres and styles they explore would mean various genres and styles of music they listen to, learn, and are able to play; these will be their repertoire because they are expected to be able to skillfully and confidently play new songs and even old popular songs. Musical genres and styles recommended for your level of learning based on this course are listed below:

1. Classical: Contemporary classical, Baroque, Romantic, etc.
2. Electronics: Ambient, House, and Techno
3. Jazz: Swing, Bepob, Cool Jazz, Fusion, etc.
4. Blues: Delta Blues, Chicago Blues, Electric Blues
5. Pop: Pop Ballads, Dance-Pop, Synthpop
6. Rock: Classic Rock, Alternative Rock, Indie Rock
7. World: Celtic, African, Indian
8. R&B/Soul: Rhythm and Blues, Soul, Motown
9. Folk: Traditional Folk, Contemporary Folk
10. Country: Classic Country, Contemporary Country
11. Gospel: Traditional Gospel, Contemporary Gospel
12. Funk: Classic Funk, Jazz-Funk

The above are suggestions based on our experience as to what is in vogue and other genres and styles from which you can greatly benefit based on their musical arrangements and chord progressions

How to Develop a Solid Repertoire?

Developing a solid repertoire isn't rocket science, nor is it magic. I cannot stress enough how important it is to listen to songs from various genres and styles. By doing this daily, you are laying a solid foundation for building your repertoire. Also, it is worth saying that though merely listening to music has many advantages for you, you still won't be maximizing the advantage if you don't score or rehearse these songs on your piano. A quick cheat for you to learn songs well and get better within very short periods at this level is to be ready to download musical sheets or chord progressions of music so that you can score the songs exactly the way the chord progressions and notes were played. You are building your repertoire.

You cant jump into expertise, you must build your repertoire over the years.

Start with simple genres with simple chords you have learned in this course. Start with simple genres and simple chords you have learned in this course In fact, by the time you follow all the advice given to you in the previous chapters and you do the practices attached to each level, you are bound to have developed a solid though basic foundation for a solid repertoire.

OTHER ESSENTIAL TOPICS FOR INTERMEDIATE PLAYERS

These other topics should be a great edge for you since these topics are usually taught at the beginning stage for professional piano players; see them as some steps early ahead into becoming a professional player. We will explain two of the topics in this unit and others in the next. The two topics are the concept of rhythm and the concept of phrasing and articulation in piano playing. Let's start one after the other

What is Rhythm?

Rhythm in piano playing is used to create structure and coherence and to express emotions in music. It is very essential to understand rhythm as a piano player. One of the fundamentals of piano playing alongside melody, harmony, and timber is rhythm to a pianist. To simplify the meaning of rhythm, it is about the duration or timing of notes and how they are placed within a musical beat or pulse. The beat is the foundation of rhythm.

A beat is a regular and recurring pulse that is often represented by either a metronome or a time signature. For example, you can have something like 4/4 or 3/4, etc. This indicates the number of beats and notes value that should receive the beats.

The concept of rhythm is realized via the precise timing and duration of each note. Pianist strictly follows the specific moments of timing required for each note to be stroked by their fingers to realize rhythms indicated in the musical notations.

Playing rhythms on the piano requires you to have a very strong sense of internal purpose and timing. You are advised to constantly practice with a metronome to develop a steady tempo and to practice various songs with various tempos and rhythms to increase your accuracy and coordination.

Lastly, you should know that rhythm is a fundamental aspect of piano playing that requires you to take caution about the organization of musical sounds and their timing. It involves being coordinated physically, having mental focus, and having salient perception to perfectly and correctly execute the indicated rhythms you see in a piece or musical notation.

Below are a few examples of the most common rhythms for you to study and develop based on the explanations given so far, and most especially through practice.

Examples of Common Rhythms and Explanation

1. Straight rhythm: This is also known as "even rhythm." It is a very common rhythm. It means playing notes evenly on each beat. You can find this type of rhythm in rock and march music.

2. Dotted Rhythm: These rhythms consist of a note followed by a dot and a not shorter than the previous. The dot tells you that the note duration is increased or extended by half to create a longer and shorter note.

3. Syncopation: This is when solid accents are placed on either off-beats or weak beats, creating a sense of tension and interest in the rhythm.

4. Rubato: This is a situation whereby the tempo is slowed for expressive purposes. Rubato is often used in music that is romantic with the interest of adding emotional depth and performance freedom to the piano player.

5. Swing Rhythm: This involves altering the timing of eight notes, having the first note quite longer than the next (the second). It is common in jazz and big bands music. Etc.

Note: We still have many more rhythms in piano playing. You may even need to review your knowledge about this concept in your beginner course in case you still need to remember it. You are advised also to review your knowledge of time signature.

You are to use the knowledge to relate to rhythm on the keyboard because you will be required to be able to count beats to know the timing for notes and chords to play, to create the desired rhythms as stated in your musical sheets or pieces.

Phrasing and articulation

Phrasing and articulation are very important subjects. Phrasing and articulation have to do with how a piece of music is interpreted, how expression is given to a piece of music, and how music is performed. We said earlier that one of the visible and important differences between a basic piano player and an intermediate piano player is the ability to express desired emotions and feelings with music. An intermediate player gives expressions and emotions to music or a piece beyond the white and black keys on the piano. Check for further explanations below to understand what they mean to and for your level.

What is Phrasing?

When we talk about phrasing, we are talking about creating a sense of musical continuity, expressions, and meanings via shaping of musical phrases or group notes. Or we can explain phrasing as shaping music into a coherent unit that convey the desired feelings and musical intentions of the player or the composer. You should see "phrasing" in music as the Language of the music because it has a beginning, middle, and end structure to communicate certain desired emotions and feelings that a player or composer wants to evoke from the audience. Phrasing helps to highlight musical structure and to convey the exact emotional content embedded in the music.

What is Articulation?

Like phrasing, articulation is very essential too in piano playing and music. It shapes the overall sound and character of the music. It refers to how notes are played and connected or how they are separated from each other. It also involves aspects such as legato (smooth and connected), staccato (short and detached), etc. You, as a pianist and, of course, as an intermediate piano player, should know that you can and should deploy articulation to express the mood, styles, and emotions of a piece or composition. Good use of articulation will help you to highlight important musical elements and create much more nuance with expressive performances to capture the essence of a piece, music, or composition.

THE EAR TRAINING TECHNIQUE

The ear training technique is how we can listen to musical notes, chords, scales, etc. We recognize and, by extension, can play the same thing even when we do not see what the pianist played. We rely on our hearing to pick sounds and discern the notes, chords, rhythms, etc., as the case may be. So, let's dive in to answer some important questions that will help you effectively play by hearing.

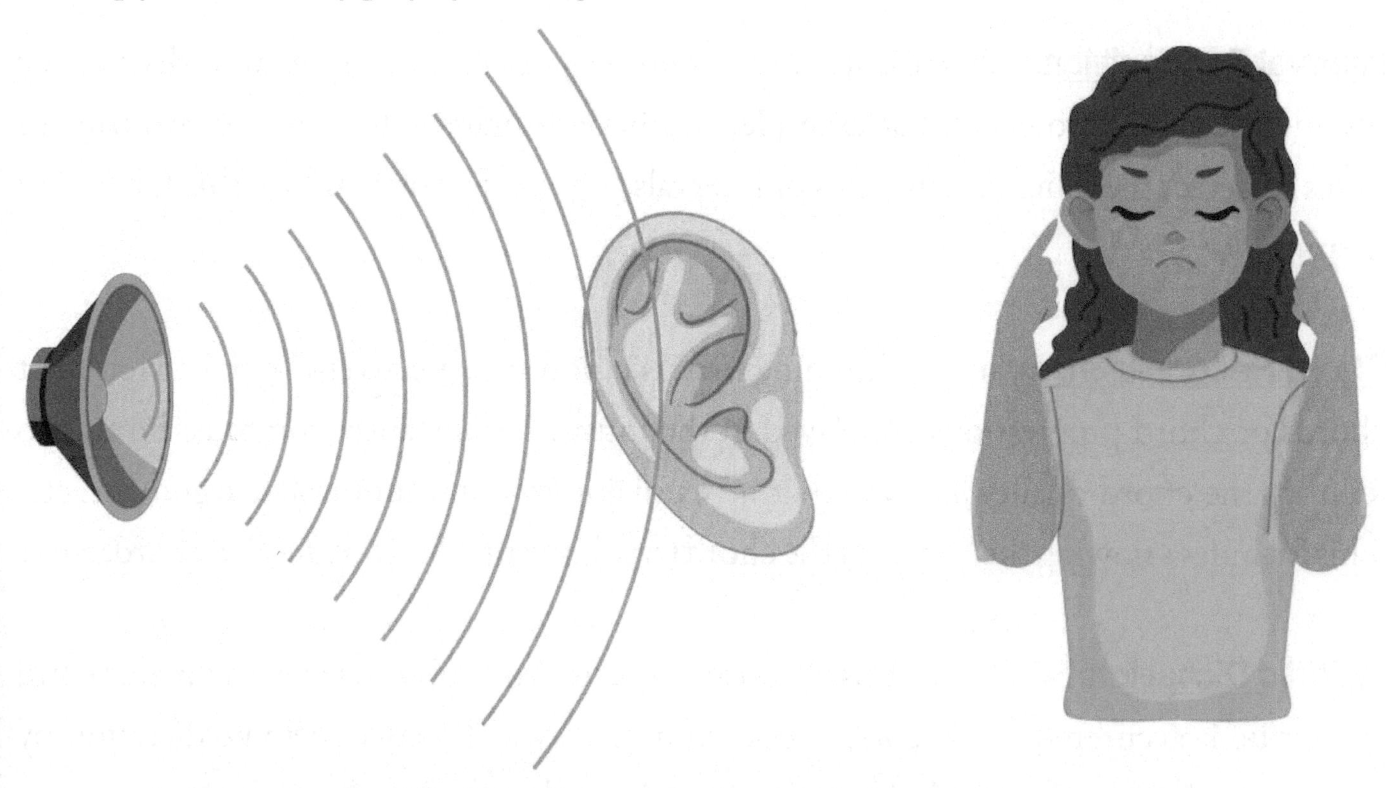

What is Ear Training in Piano Playing?

Ear training is as vital as every other basic skill you need to possess as an intermediate piano player. Ear training is a musical education that helps piano players develop their ability to recognize, interpret, and play musical elements like musical pitches, chords, rhythms, and intervals by ear. It would help you play correct and accurate music if you were equipped with this skill as an intermediate piano player. It will also enable you transcribe songs to tonic sofas or notes, and compose music. Below are some examples of ear training techniques on the piano.

Ear Training Techniques

We have several ear training techniques in music. These ear training techniques are created and designed to enhance the sharpness of your listening skills and improve your ability to recognize and reproduce or teach the same musical elements correctly and accurately. I highlighted for you some important ear training techniques that will help you and your "listening-playing" below.

Interval Recognition: By this, we mean training your ears to know and identify the distance between two notes. For example, you have to practice listening to two pairs of notes to detect the difference in terms of intervals (e.g., perfect fifth, minor third) between them.

Chord Recognition: By merely listening to music, you are expected to be able to tell what chords or chord progressions are played in the music. For instance, you must be able to identify the chord quality, i.e., whether it is a major, minor, diminished, argument, etc. This includes knowing the "type" of the chord (triad, seventh chord, extended chord, etc.).

Melodic Dictation: By hearing music, you are expected to be able to listen to a melody and transcribe it accurately so that you can learn it or play it. Practice melodic dictation by listening to short and long melodies and writing down the notes you hear.

Sight Singing: This involves you being able to sing music from a written score without prior rehearsals. It would help if you practiced this often by singing melodies from a music score without playing them on your instrument. It will enable you get along with musical notes.

Transcription: This involves being able to listen to music and being able to list out all the notes, melodies, harmony, and rhythms in the music. You are advised to often listen to songs and get these out on paper and try to play the same thing.

Note: We still have several contents on this topic. However, everything explained above and all that ear training involved must be practiced by listening to more music and trying to do everything explained here. You are advised to commit to training your ears seriously; it is a skill you must develop at this level.

GLOSSARY

This glossary contains complex terms within the body of this course.

1. Accelerando: This refers to gradually increasing the tempo or speed of music. It is indicated in musical sheets as "accel."

2. The Cycle of Fifth: This is a sequence of musical pitches or keys, each perfect fifth lower or higher than the previous one.

3. Key Signature: A key signature is an indicator of keys on a piece and notes that should be played consistently as sharps and flats throughout the music. It is at the beginning of each staff to help you determine the key and scale of the piece.

4. Musical Sheet: A musical sheet, or sheet music, for piano, is a written or printed document that contains musical notation for a piece of music.

5. Ornaments: This is a musical embellishment or decoration added to a melody to enhance
its expressiveness and ornamentation. Ornament variants include trills, turns, mordents, and grace notes. It also adds flair and sophistication to music when played appropriately.

6. Ritardando: It is the opposite of accelerando. It indicates a gradual decrease in tempo, slowing down the pace of the music. It is often abbreviated as "rit" or "ritard." It can be used in musical pieces to create a sense of relaxation or conclusion at the end of a musical piece or phrase.

Made in the USA
Las Vegas, NV
29 November 2024